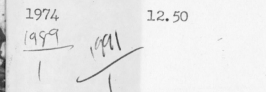

CAPTAIN SCOTT
And the Antarctic Tragedy
Peter Brent

C. 1

Saturday Review Press
New York

Designed by Sasha Rowntree *for*
George Weidenfeld and Nicolson Limited,
11 St John's Hill, London SW11 1XA
and Saturday Review Press,
201 Park Avenue South,
New York, N.Y. 10003

Filmset by Cox & Wyman Ltd,
London, Fakenham and Reading

ISBN: 0-8715-0258-7
Library of Congress Catalog
Card No: 73-75732

Printed in Great Britain

Contents

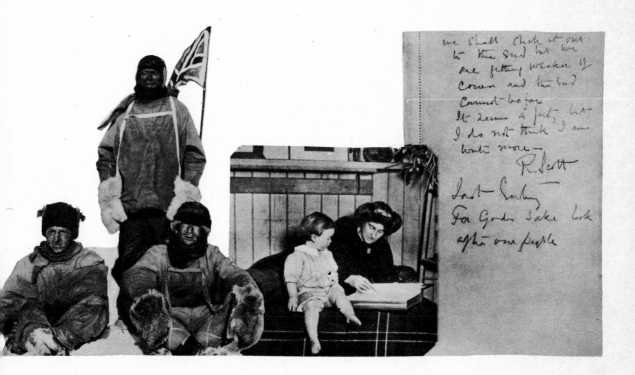

Introduction

THROUGHOUT HISTORY PEOPLE HAVE ADMIRED EXPLORERS and have wondered at accounts of their discoveries. Often they lack sufficient knowledge to make valid judgements, and sometimes they have even been misled; but they appreciate that such men have endured hardship far beyond the bounds of normal experience, and for this they are esteemed. Many names from the past are known throughout the world and many more have their own particular national aura and importance. Robert Falcon Scott comes into both categories and perhaps it is not too much to suggest that his story has become part of the world's heritage.

Scott had those qualities of dedication, endurance and determination which singled him out from his fellows. These characteristics and his achievements in the face of constant hardships are what remain, and should continue to remain, in the community memory as an example to succeeding generations of an ordinary, fallible man's mastery of himself and triumph over adversity. He was a successful naval officer, he was deeply in love, at times he made errors of judgement, he suffered from doubts, and perhaps too from occasional jealousies – these are the attributes which make up the ordinary man. It is when they are discarded or disregarded, and still there remains a substantial figure, that we recognise his qualification to a niche in the halls of fame.

In this book the essentials of the Scott story are vividly portrayed. At the same time we find revealed the differences of thought and community attitudes between this generation and those who lived immediately after the reign of Queen Victoria. National pride, high standards of upright behaviour, and the application of community and personal discipline have today

Introduction

all lost some of their appeal. In judging Scott, however, we should remember the criteria of his period and not apply today's standards to an era for which they are inappropriate. Indeed, we may even question whether all the changes in attitudes which have come about so rapidly are necessarily for the better; this perhaps is something which is highlighted in the following chapters.

Another aspect of the difference between the Scott period and present times lies in the materials and techniques used in polar work. In the early years of the century we had little knowledge of Antarctic conditions and there were no proved techniques of successful travel. Modern exploration owes a great debt to those who pioneered the early techniques and suffered severely in gaining experience the hard way. It is all too easy to criticise them with hindsight and in the light of technical advances beyond their wildest dreams. There is no doubt that Scott was alive to the need to try out new equipment, for he took south first a captive balloon for air reconnaissance, and then the early tractors for hauling loads. In the event neither proved satisfactory and he had to fall back on the traditional means of transport – dogs, ponies and man-hauling.

Today it is difficult to understand how anyone could believe that ponies could be successful in the Antarctic, but it was still the horse era, and they were known to be used in Manchuria. One may perhaps be more critical of the failure to gain expertise in dog-driving, especially as he had more than once consulted Nansen and knew how successful the Norwegians were in this respect. Indeed, it was this very fact which enabled Amundsen to beat him to the Pole. But Scott shared the British passion for animals and could not bear to use them ruthlessly or cause them suffering. There was always the reliable technique of man-hauling to fall back on, and one suspects that ponies, tractors and dogs were not really a very serious part of his plan. It is perhaps ironical that the British have now learnt how to manage dogs without causing them to suffer, and are the last nation still to use them in the Antarctic. It is a measure of their reliability that they remain the safest form of transport in dangerous areas, and enable us to work in places inaccessible to modern tractors.

In the end it was the terrible physical demands of man-hauling which caused the loss of the Polar Party. The question is often asked whether Scott's last expedition would have achieved the fame it did, and stood so high in the nation's eyes, if they had survived. Perhaps not – but they still would have deserved recognition for a prodigious feat of endurance which should still make us feel proud. Their journey was not merely a follow-up of someone else's previous achievement, but began before, and in time ran side-by-side with, the successful Amundsen expedition. That they died after reaching their goal added an emotional aura which even compensated for the loss of the race. This is exemplified by the generous gesture of the United States when their station, established in 1956 at the South Pole, was named Amundsen/Scott Station.

V. E. Fuchs

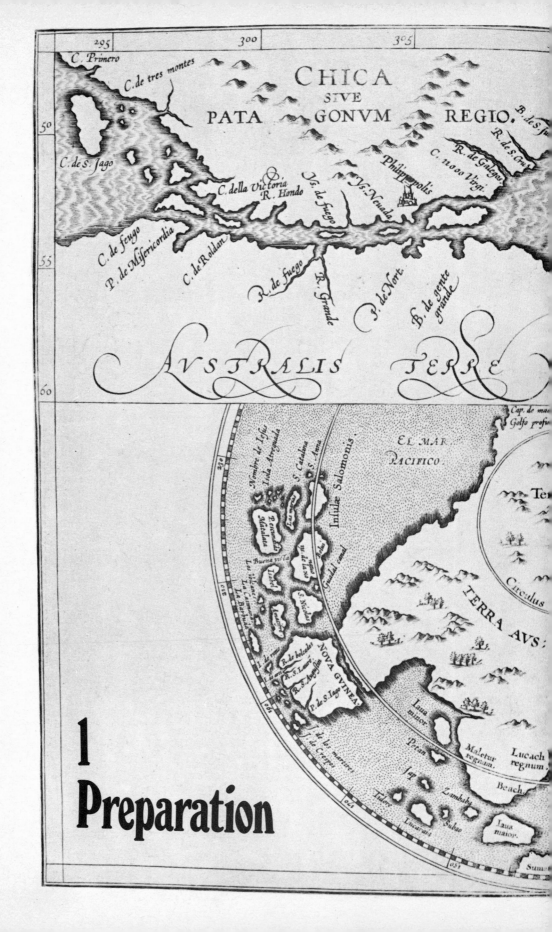

1
Preparation

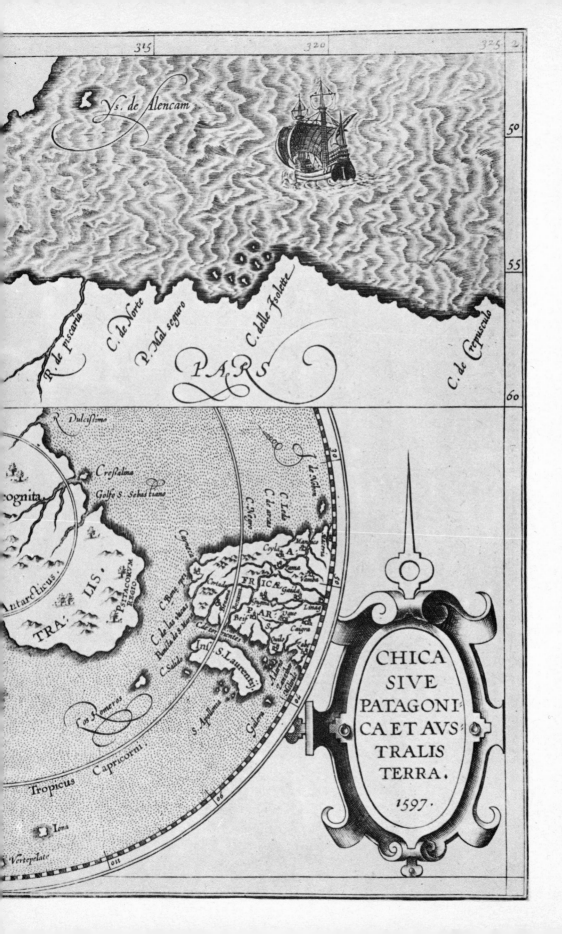

Ys. de Alencam

50

55

R. de piscaria

C. de Norte

P. Mal seguro

C. delle Isolette

C. de Crepusculo

P A R S

60

R. Dulcissimo

Crestalina

Golfo S. Sebastiano

cognita

Antarcticus.

TRA . LIS.

PSITACORVM REGIO

Capraia

C. de Salas

C. Nigro

C. de arcas

C. Leli

S. de Salas

Manfico A.

Coyla

Roma

Vamba

Gaida

Linag

Vine

Caigra

FR ICA

PAR

Brig

Quilo

F

C. Bons

C. de las obras

Rueda de 9 Nom

C. de Ladrones

Inf. S. Laurentij

C. Salda

Los Romeros

Tropicus Capricorni.

S. Apollonia

Galipa

Iona

S Vertepelate

CHICA SIVE PATAGONI CA ET AVS TRALIS TERRA. 1597 .

As a child, and perhaps always, he was something of a dreamer; his father used to call him 'Old Mooney'. Less impressive than the full name, Robert Falcon Scott, which seems so appropriate in restrospect, those close to him always called him 'Con'. Early, there seemed little in him of the stuff of heroes. He hated the sight of blood, which until manhood made him sick. When it was first thought that he would make the Navy his career, the local doctor who examined him was discouraging – the boy, he said, would never be big enough in chest and shoulders. Yet there was, in Nelsonian manner, another side to him. He cut himself badly with his first penknife but, disdaining sympathy or scorn, surmounting his horror of blood, he put his hand in his pocket and walked away, a stubborn seven-year-old pretending unconcern. By the time he was eight, a self-appointed 'admiral', he led his brother and his sisters on the miniature campaigns and expeditions of childhood. Once, after some trial and error, he devised a charge of gunpowder and blew a plank (to him a battleship, the *Terror of Devon*) out of the local stream.

He was thus controlled, complex, already something of a leader; but there was nothing then that suggested he would become a candidate for fame. No one saw those qualities in him until 1887 when, a young lieutenant not yet twenty, he was singled out by Sir Clements Markham as a possible future leader for the Antarctic ventures that patriotic geographer was already obsessedly planning. Even then, it was to be another twelve years before Scott himself would realise that he had been so picked out and, responding to the choice, would find himself on the road to his ambivalent destiny.

Scott was born on 6 June 1868 in Devonport. Despite his West-country birth he believed himself to be descended from the Border clan of Scotts, men who had fought over the wind-clipped hills between England and Scotland for generations, until the Stuart rising of 1745, their last and most aggressive fling, scattered them and drained their power. Certainly his direct ancestor, Robert Scott, arrived in Devonshire from France, appearing from that Jacobite haven in 1780 with stories of an uncle hanged after Culloden. More notably Sir Walter Scott, the great Romantic novelist, loomed in his ancestry; the connection was a family myth which is almost proved by the resemblance Con himself, and several other men of the family, bore to that famous writer.

PREVIOUS PAGES Map of Antarctica published in 1597.

12

Scott aged 6 with his brother Archie.

The family lived in a comfortable house, Outlands, standing in a couple of acres of garden and copse, which Con's grandfather had bought nearly fifty years before. When he was eight, young Robert Scott went out into the world for the first time, progressing from governesses at home to Exmouth House, a day school at Stoke Damarel. He made the daily journey on a rather fiery little pony named Beppo; once, when it bolted, he walked the seven miles home but took care, with promising practicality, to give Beppo's description to every police station he passed. When he was thirteen, he was sent to Stubbington House in Fareham, a Hampshire school where he prepared for the Royal Navy's cadetship examinations. Stubbington House – or Foster's, the name it took from its proprietor – was one of a handful of schools cramming boys for the next stage of their

13

The *Discovery* Expedition

ss *Discovery* was built especially for the National Antarctic Expedition of 1901-4; although wooden-built, and thus very different from today's specially designed steel-reinforced ships, she nevertheless thrust through the ice-bound seas of the Antarctic with great success. Powered by engines auxiliary to sails, bound in timbers of oak and elm, her strengthened stem was designed to ride up over and crush the ice; an overhanging, rounded stern protected the rudder and screw. The living accommodation was adapted for the cold with double doors and skylights, and lagging under the decks. There was storage space for two years' supplies.

"DISCOVERY"

THE

SOUTH POLAR TIMES.

APRIL · 1902

LEFT Title page to the first edition of *The South Polar Times*, the periodical edited by Shackleton and illustrated by Wilson.
ABOVE Watercolour by Edward Wilson of the *Discovery*.
RIGHT Commemoration postcard sent on the departure of the *Discovery* from England.

BRITISH NATIONAL ANTARCTIC EXPEDITION, 1901.

ANTARCTIC
EXPᴰⁿ
1901
S.S. DISCOVERY

COMMANDER SCOTT, R.N.

THE "DISCOVERY."

Valentine.

"When Drake went down to the Horn
. . . England was crowned thereby,
'Twixt seas unsailed and shores unhailed,
England was crowned thereby.
As now we witness here,
While men depart, of joyful heart,
Adventure for to know."—*Kipling.*

God be with you.
Your's Ted.
the Cape

This card, commemorating the departure of the Expedition, was posted from London the day
the S.S. "Discovery" sailed.

Oct. 3. '01.

The Scott family's claim to connections with the famous writer, Sir Walter Scott (left), is borne out by the close resemblance to him of several men of the family, including Robert Falcon Scott himself (right).

naval education, in HMS *Britannia*, the celebrated training ship. The level of education expected was quite high, equivalent to four years in a public school, which made *Britannia* a sort of junior maritime university.

With her tall foremast, her jib-boom and flying jib on which the boys were unofficially expected to display their nerve, *Britannia* lay anchored in the River Dart. Education there was concentrated mostly on seamanship, as was only natural; mathematics sufficient for navigation was also taught, as was some French. More academic subjects were treated with an authoritarian disdain. In 1883 Scott graduated with first-class certificates in mathematics and seamanship, seventh in a class of twenty-six. He was ready to move on once more, out into the mainstream of a naval career; he became a midshipman, a 'snottie', in HMS *Boadicea*.

16

Later he served in *Lion* and in *Monarch* and decided to specialise as a torpedo officer. Joining the West Indies Training Squadron, he was appointed to HMS *Rover*. The year was 1887; circumstances had brought him to a time and place crucial for the working out of his fate, for the cousin of the Squadron Commodore was Sir Clements Markham, Honorary Secretary and later President of the Royal Geographical Society. Having once served in the Navy, he had retained a life-long interest in it; now he was on a visit to his cousin and already scanning the midshipmen in training for potential leaders of Antarctic expeditions. For Sir Clements, Antarctica was the last arena in which manhood, British manhood and, specifically, that manhood nurtured and developed by the Royal Navy, might conclusively try itself. He felt that in so bleak a continent, dominated as it was by conditions utterly inimical to humanity, humanity

Outlands, Scott's family home in Devonport, Devonshire.

17

had found its ultimate proving ground. The scientific discoveries which might be made there were to him of secondary importance; perhaps for Scott, too, it was this romantic view which was later to prevail, but he always insisted on the scientific value of his expeditions.

Markham, a man of great energy and tenacity of purpose, was scrutinising the young officers for the human material he would need when the time came to send off the expeditions he had long envisaged. The men he wanted, he wrote in the notes he was steadily compiling, should be young:

> The fatal mistake, in selecting commanders for former polar expeditions, has been to seek for experience instead of youth. Both cannot be united, and youth is absolutely essential ... Elderly men are not accessible to new ideas and have not the energy and capacity necessary to meet emergencies. How can novel forms of effort be expected from stiff old organisms hampered by experience!

With this in mind, and realising that the time when he would need them might still be long in coming, he watched the young midshipmen around him with great attention. 'Allowing for the changes wrought by a dozen years', he wrote, 'I believed Tommy Smyth to be the best man in the *Active*, though wanting ballast, Hyde Parker in the *Volage*, and Robert F. Scott in the *Rover*.' After dining at the Commodore's table he wrote, more definitely, 'Noel, his Captain, who rarely praised anyone, spoke highly of Scott. ... My final conclusion was that Scott was the destined man to command the Antarctic expedition.' He was then nineteen. (Later, however, in a list under the heading 'Possible Antarctic Leaders', Markham placed Scott's name, without comment, sixth out of eleven.)

Unaware that in a sense the rest of his life had already been planned and decided, Scott moved one rung up the ladder he thought he had chosen to mount; in August 1887 he was commissioned as a sub-lieutenant and a year later was posted to HMS *Amphion*. Ordered to join her at Esquimault, British Columbia, Scott found himself aboard a tramp steamer out of San Francisco, travelling north in a full gale. An Englishman named Courtauld Thomson (a Red Cross administrator who became Lord Courtauld-Thomson) wrote later:

> Then it was I first knew Con Scott was no ordinary human being. Though at that time still only a boy, he practically took command of the passengers. ... With a small body of volunteers he ... dressed the

mothers, washed the children, fed the babies, swabbed down the floors and nursed the sick. . . . On deck he settled the quarrels and established order by his personality, or, if necessary, by his fists.

The qualities he displayed when unexpectedly challenged by circumstance in this way held good in a more pacific environment too – in 1891 he gained the necessary certificates to rise one rank, to full lieutenant, obtaining the highest marks of his year for seamanship, and later passing his examinations at the Royal

Scott as a lieutenant, the rank he attained in 1891.

19

Scott's mother, to whom he showed devoted concern all his life.

Naval College, Greenwich, first out of a class of nineteen. With these qualifications behind him, he settled for the next three years at Plymouth, stationed at the torpedo school there and thus able to spend many of his leaves at his Devonport home.

A little later in that last decade of the century, however, Scott's fortunes changed. His father, owner of the family brewery, had for a long time managed to keep it going only with great difficulty; now he was forced to sell it and try and find work as a manager in some more successful establishment. Outlands had to be let. Scott was faced with having to keep up appearances as an officer on less than £200 a year. There seems no question that he found the restrictions this imposed on him irksome, accepting as he did so completely the ideals and conventions of a period which thought poverty not merely a misfortune but almost immoral.

The family moved, then scattered. Scott's sisters marched cheerfully out into the world of work – one became a nurse, another an actress, the other two began a dressmaking business in Chelsea. His brother, an army subaltern, joined a West African regiment, thus limiting his expenditure. Scott himself pursued ambitions which, with hindsight, we see as strangely modest. He wanted, he wrote to his father, to be known as 'a competent torpedo man'. Although he would have liked rapid promotion, he was not avidly ambitious; he recognised too that he was in a Service where those with powerful family connections stood a better chance than he did. He writes of the son of the Earl of Derby, a godson of Victoria, and of the son of an admiral, both applying for a posting he would have liked: 'All these people will try for the billet – so you see I fear there is a very poor chance for me.' It is not clear whether he felt any bitterness over this, although given his general acceptance of the prevailing ideas of his time, it is unlikely. It would be a rare naval officer who, during the late-Victorian era, permitted himself in any way to challenge the established social order.

In 1897 Scott suffered a double blow. His father, who had been ill for some time, finally died. And, perhaps the more grievous loss, his brother Archie, home on leave, suddenly developed typhoid fever and died within a week. In a family which had always been close-knit, where for example the two brothers had without question taken up the burden of supporting those who needed support, most notably their mother, this must have been hard for Scott to bear. From Gibraltar, where he was serving as torpedo officer in HMS *Majestic*, he wrote to his mother, 'It is good to hear there was no pain and it is easy to understand that he died like a man' – a cliché which he used with a sincerity his own ending was to demonstrate.

A minor step on the way to that destined end: in the same year, 1897, he and Markham met again, the latter still thinking of his projected Antarctic explorations. 'I was more than ever impressed by his evident vocation for such a command', he wrote. Yet Scott, still ignorant of having been singled out in this way, went on with his career, serving for the next two years in

HMS *Majestic*, now the flagship of the Channel Squadron. It was not until June 1899 that, quite by chance, he met Markham in the street and learned of that determined man's long-standing intention. In his book *The Voyage of the 'Discovery'* Scott tells how, 'chancing one day to walk down Buckingham Palace Road, I espied Sir Clements on the opposite pavement, and naturally crossed, and as naturally turned and accompanied him to his house. That afternoon I learned for the first time that there was

Sir Clements Markham, the powerful personality behind both of Scott's Antarctic expeditions and the man responsible for selecting Scott as their leader.

such a thing as a prospective Antarctic expedition; two days later I wrote applying to command it, and a year after that I was officially appointed.'

In 1860 the Superintendent of the Hydrographic Branch of the United States Navy, Captain Mathew Fontaine Maury, read a paper on Antarctic exploration to the Royal Geographical Society. Suggesting that a winter base could be set up from which local expeditions might set forth by boat or over the ice, he pointed out that most of the continental mass of Antarctica was 'as little known as the interior of the moon'.

Ten years later, under the auspices of the Royal Society and the Admiralty, HMS *Challenger*, a wooden, steam-driven corvette of 2000 tons, set out on what was to become one of the most significant oceanographic surveys the world has ever seen. In the course of this, two years and two months after her departure from England, *Challenger* crossed the Antarctic Circle and for a month took sights and soundings in those bleak seas. From the sea-bed she dredged up boulders, great stones carried far from their places of origin, first by glaciers and later by the huge icebergs which broke away, floated for a while, then began to break up and melt, depositing on the silt fathoms below their pieces of invaluable geological evidence. For evidence is what these rock samples proved to be, pointers to the nature and structure of an uninviting and largely invisible continent. This was made plain in a lecture given by Sir John Murray to the Royal Geographical Society in 1893. Murray, who had been biologist in the *Challenger*, had spent the intervening twenty years collating and publishing the results of that survey. Now he had finished his work on the south polar regions, and there is no doubt that his reconstruction from this and even thinner evidence of the profile of Antarctica excited the interest and speculation of his audience. Addressing himself ·to this excitement, Murray pleaded for a programme of Antarctic exploration, a field which had been left largely to the incidental observations of such British and Norwegian whalers as had crossed its maritime frontiers in search of their disappearing prey.

It was the Norwegians, however, who in 1893 sent the whaling ship *Antarctic* on a voyage of polar discovery. Some fifteen months later men for the first time stood on the Antarctic continent, landing near that Cape Adare which Sir James Clark

Ross had seen over half a century before and named after the Member of Parliament for Glamorganshire. Ostensibly searching for whales, the Norwegians nevertheless wrote, 'we got a strong impression that the bay at Cape Adare . . . would provide many advantages as a landing place and station for the new expedition.'

In 1897 the Belgians promoted an expedition, sending out a naval lieutenant, Adrien de Gerlache, in a Norwegian sealer named *Belgica*. Her first mate was a Norwegian, as yet unknown – Roald Amundsen. In March of the following year *Belgica* found herself trapped in the ice throughout the permanent night of the Antarctic winter. It was not until the spring of 1899 that the ship could be sawn and blasted free.

In the meantime the *Southern Cross*, also a Norwegian whaler, had sailed from London. This expedition, however, was not financed by official or institutional funds, nor was it sponsored by any learned or governmental body. The backing for this expedition came from George Newnes, the founder of *Tit-Bits*, *Strand Magazine* and the other publications of a burgeoning magazine empire; it was led by a Norwegian named Borchgrevink, a veteran of the recently returned *Antarctic* expedition, one of the men who had landed at Cape Adare. This time he took with him sledges and dog teams; for the first time men did not merely float at the edges of this ice-covered continent, or at best step timidly upon its forbidding coast, they moved with some confidence across its surface, their faces turned to the south. It was in February 1900 that Borchgrevink landed on the Ross Ice Shelf: 'At this place I effected a landing with sledges, dogs, provisions and instruments; and leaving the vessel with the rest of the expedition . . . I myself, accompanied by Lieutenant Colbeck and the Finn Savio, proceeded southwards, reaching 78°50'S, the furthest south ever reached by man.' That was all he told the Royal Geographical Society about his journey when he lectured them in London; but there the phrase stands, ready to be garlanded by all the flags of a rampant nationalism – 'the furthest south'.

In England, meanwhile, Sir Clements Markham pursued his own plans. Because he realised that he would need not only the patriotism which had for over a century lent its energy to exploration and annexation throughout the world, but also the support of the scientific establishment, he engineered an alliance between his own Royal Geographical Society and the Royal

OPPOSITE Roald Amundsen, the Norwegian explorer, whose party was to be the first to reach the South Pole, four weeks ahead of Scott.

Society, that austere, august body, fellowship of which guarantees any British scientist an ultimate and unchallengeable prestige.

Almost at once, however, disagreements appeared over the leadership and manning of the planned expedition. Sir John Murray, spokesman for the Royal Society, had already declared, 'A dash for the South Pole is not ... what British science at the present time desires. It demands rather a steady, continuous, laborious and systematic exploration of the whole southern region with all the appliances of the modern investigator.' So cool an approach was itself at the opposite pole from the romantic if determined approach of Sir Clements. Murray, for his purposes, needed a civilian leader, one trained in some suitable discipline, preferably an academic. Markham, on the other hand, with the higher echelons of the Royal Geographical Society stuffed with admirals, wanted to see the expedition led and manned by naval men, disciplined, durable and certain of their patriotic priorities.

Money too became a point of contention. Murray argued that this should be raised first; only when the extent of their funds could be measured should the proposed expedition be equipped. Markham, who had been toying with plans for this venture over some twenty years, disagreed; oddly impetuous, he maintained that if there were enough money to equip one ship, that should be done, rather than waiting to equip two as had been planned. Success would lead to enthusiasm and enthusiasm to further funds. Failure or disaster, on the other hand, would force the Government to intervene in any necessary efforts to rescue marooned or ice-bound adventurers. One can imagine that this slightly speculative approach would seem dangerously unprofessional to the calculating mind of a scientist.

Despite these difficulties, however, the preparations for the expedition gained momentum. By 1899 Markham had some £15,000 at his disposal, and had made preliminary plans to co-ordinate the work of his explorers with those preparing to set out from Germany and from Sweden. His hopes were raised when further large sums were made available, notably from the industrialist, Llewellyn Longstaff, and the newspaper proprietor, Alfred Harmsworth (later Lord Northcliffe). His fund now at the very promising level of £45,000, Markham approached the Government, who had until then been rather

OPPOSITE Carsten Borchgrevink, the Norwegian leader of the British expedition of 1898-1900, famous for his use of dogs and for the first claim to have reached the 'furthest south'.

BELOW Lord Northcliffe, founder of the *Daily Mail*, whose financial backing helped greatly to launch the *Discovery* expedition.

ostentatiously lukewarm. Faced by the public's gathering enthusiasm, however, the Treasury agreed to double the amount at the expedition's disposal.

With money at last available, work could begin in earnest. A Ship Committee had been formed; it now decided that the expedition's vessel should be built in Dundee, her design similar to that of a rebuilt whaler which had taken part in the British Government's Arctic Expedition of 1875. That ship had been the *Discovery*, the fifth of the name to take part in a programme of official exploration; the first had sailed to Hudson Bay and Baffin Bay as early as 1601. It was decided that Scott's new ship should be the sixth in this lineage – as he wrote, 'the heir to a long record of honourable service, and, what was equally important, of fortunate service, as the name *Discovery* seems never to have been associated with shipwreck or disaster'. She had a registered tonnage of 485, was 172 feet long, 34 feet in breadth. She was, he wrote, 'a splendidly strong and well-fortified structure, and the machinery was in all respects equal to the hull'.

Scott, while all these preparations were in hand, remained at sea in *Majestic*, waiting while Markham struggled with committees and meetings, with minutes and reports – 'harder to force a way through than the most impenetrable of ice-packs', as he himself put it – until Scott's appointment as expedition leader was at last confirmed. 'On June 30, 1900,' he tells us, 'I was promoted to the rank of commander, and a month later my duties in the *Majestic* lapsed, and I was free to undertake the work of the expedition. The year which followed was in many respects the busiest I have ever spent. . . .'

First he decided that he should repair his own deficiencies as expedition leader – as he tells us himself, 'I may as well confess that I have no predilection for polar exploration.' He therefore went to see the one man who indisputably did, Fridtjof Nansen the Norwegian, travelling to Christiana (now Oslo) with Sir Clements Markham in order to discover above all the secrets of that skill at which Nansen had become particularly expert, sledging. The stay was short for Nansen was always a busy man, preparing his own expeditions and bearing as best he could the burdens of fame. Scott wrote that 'it was impossible not to realise that one was robbing him of hours which he could ill afford to spare'; soon he was on his way to confer with Professor von Drygalski in Berlin. Under the Professor, the Germans were

OPPOSITE Fridtjof Nansen, Norwegian explorer and expert with dog teams, whose advice that they be used was to prove tragically correct.

29

also mounting an expedition, its schedule setting a sailing date very close to Scott's own. It was with astonishment that Scott saw how far advanced von Drygalski's preparations were: 'I was forced to realise that this was all in marked contrast with the state of things in England, and I hastened home in considerable alarm.' The fact that a Swedish expedition under Nordenskjöld was already asking for coaling facilities in the Falkland Islands can hardly have helped restore his equanimity. Even Scotland, his ancestral motherland, was mounting an Antarctic venture of its own, under Dr W.S.Bruce, and had asked the Admiralty for the loan of specialised scientific instruments. It was as if the South Pole and its ice-covered continental mass had been chosen as one theatre in which the dramas of European national rivalry were to be played out.

While the new *Discovery* was building in Dundee, Scott turned to the problems of manning his expedition. 'From a very early date', he wrote later, 'I had set my mind on obtaining a naval crew. I felt sure that their sense of discipline would be an immense acquisition, and I had grave doubt as to my own ability to deal with any other class of men.' He had, of course, for most of his life been either preparing for or living in a naval environment, and it is not surprising that rather than leave it for this new venture he would have preferred to extend it, making his new life another version of the old. While he tried to argue the Admiralty into lending him the men he wanted, he began recruiting his officers.

In addition to what might be termed the executive arm of the expedition, scientists would also be needed; these eventually included two doctors, a biologist, a geologist and a physicist. From their ranks Scott found the man who became the one he most admired and depended on during his explorations: Edward Wilson, a doctor who was also a zoologist and, more particularly, a fine draughtsman and painter. On the other hand, among the officers, he took on as third mate Ernest Shackleton, who over the next few years would emerge as his greatest British rival; there seems no question that, while Scott and Shackleton respected each other, they were men of very different stamp between whom relations were always at least potentially abrasive.

Wilson was some four years younger than Scott. He had studied at Cambridge and trained at St George's Hospital. His face suggests the strength he was always to display, yet it is

OPPOSITE Dr Edward Wilson photographed in the Antarctic; a remarkable and talented man who justly deserved the love and respect shown to him by those around him. He wrote of himself, 'I don't feel built at all for today's bustle and push.'

strangely fine-drawn, with a sensitive mouth: he has the features of the artist, the intellectual. And his strength was not merely that which underlay his physical endurance, but was also displayed in his morality, his sense of honour, which to some extent Scott and others were to use as a yardstick by which they would measure their own behaviour.

Shackleton was a very different kind of man. He was an officer in the Merchant Marine, introduced by Markham into the expedition, a man who radiated strength and energy. Of Anglo-Irish stock, he had been all his life something of a rolling stone. He claimed to have run away to sea, with his savings and the works of his favourite poet, Browning, in his pocket; in fact, more prosaically, he was decently apprenticed at the age of sixteen to the North-Western Shipping Company. His father, a doctor with a large number of children, had not had the means to put his son through the protracted training of a naval officer. Shackleton served in several ships and worked for several lines, gaining his master's ticket in the process. On a voyage to the Cape, he had become friendly with the son of that Llewellyn Longstaff whose generosity had helped Markham to make the expedition a reality; now it was through Longstaff that he found himself introduced to Sir Clements and to Scott. Broad-shouldered, out-going, loquacious, with a touch of the Irish brogue always in his speech, he had an engaging, easy-going manner which must have found the naval discipline Scott was to insist on a little irksome. His position once regularised by his being commissioned into the Royal Naval Reserve, however, Shackleton seems to have found no difficulty in becoming, and being accepted as, one of the chosen team. Nevertheless, Markham's notes bear witness to the change of opinion he went through over his expedition's third mate; the complimentary, 'He is a steady, high-principled young man' was later altered to the lukewarm, 'He seemed a steady young man'. More damagingly, the original enthusiastic opening remark, 'Scott was fortunate in finding such an excellent and zealous officer for third lieutenant', was changed to the mere, 'Scott appointed Ernest Shackleton to be third executive officer'.

Other officers joined, each carefully vetted by Scott. He worked twelve hours a day in a small office in Burlington House, surrounded by pieces of equipment, clothing and tinned food. He struggled, sometimes less than adequately because of his lack of administrative experience, with the logistic problems

A silhouette of Ernest Shackleton drawn by Edward Wilson.

which arise in endless droves at this stage of an expedition's preparation. Nansen had warned him that the most important element in exploration was getting together the right supplies and equipment, and he applied himself conscientiously to this task. In *The Voyage of the 'Discovery'* he lists the sometimes unexpected items with which he had to be concerned: boatswain's stores, carpenter's stores, engineer's stores, ice implements, explosives for blowing a path through the ice fields, tobacco, soap, crockery, mattresses, oil lamps, stoves, candles, medicines, cameras, a library; all this apart from the major items like canvas boats, prefabricated huts for the shore base, scientific

The officers and crew of the *Discovery*
photographed on deck before sailing.

34

Plumley.

'ild. Croucher. Kennar. Handsley. Lashly. Crean. Dell. Evans Clarke. Weller

ilbeam. Joyce. Williamson. Heald. Cross. Smythe. Scott.

Dr. Wilson. Lt. Eng. Skelton. Lt. Royds. Dr. Koettlitz. Mr. Ferrar. Dellbridge.

Capt. Scott. Mr. Bernacchi. Mr. Hodgson. Dailey.

instruments of all kinds – 'and so on almost *ad infinitum*', as he rather wearily brings this account to an end.

At the same time he was involved in a dispute with the expedition's scientific leader, the geologist J. W. Gregory, a professor on leave of absence from Melbourne University. Gregory had been surprised, even outraged, at discovering that he and those working to his direction were to be placed under Scott's command. It may well be that under those circumstances he found the idea of the naval discipline Scott was to impose rather restricting. As he wrote to the Royal Society's representatives on the expedition's Joint Committee, 'there would be no guarantee to prevent the scientific work from being subordinated to naval adventure'. More specifically, he complained a little later that Scott had ordered scientific instruments without consulting him – perhaps a petty quibble, yet, if true, one suggesting at least thoughtlessness on Scott's part. Tension reached the point at which Gregory felt forced to resign; two members of the Joint Committee took the same course.

The antagonism this dispute had stirred up between the Royal Society and the Royal Geographical Society carried over into another argument. While the Royal Society wanted Scott to be instructed not to winter on the ice unless he absolutely could not avoid doing so, the Royal Geographical Society wanted the matter left entirely to Scott's judgement. An arbitration committee of six, three from each Society, agreed that the decision should be left to Scott.

On 21 March 1901 *Discovery* was launched and sent ceremoniously down the slipway by Lady Markham. Partly fitted out, she was towed to London and, early in June that year, secured to a jetty in East India Dock. As the expedition's supplies were loaded, the men who were to use them slowly assembled. The Admiralty had given way on the number of their personnel who were to make the voyage; in the end only nine of the forty-eight members were not either officers, non-commissioned officers or ratings in the Royal Navy. Scott picked these men mostly from the ships he knew best, those of the Channel Squadron with which he himself had so recently seen service. As he points out, 'I had friends in each ship of this fleet to whom I could write asking them to select one or two men from those who volunteered for the service.' By this simple screening process, he seems to have obtained some guarantee of the quality of those who sailed with him, while at the same time saving himself many anxious hours of interviewing and assessment.

He also ensured that he would have no problems in imposing naval discipline in a ship which, strictly speaking, fell under the far laxer code of the Merchant Shipping Act. Scott felt, however, that the provisions of that Act 'fail to provide that guarantee for strict obedience and good behaviour which I believe to be a necessity for such exceptional conditions as exist in polar service'. Not everyone, however, would have continued to insist through three years of Antarctic blizzard, mishap, triumph and bereavement on the essential difference between the men in the officers' wardroom and those who sailed with them; only a British crew, perhaps, would have accepted such an hierarchical structure with the equanimity Scott's men displayed. 'We lived exactly as though the ship and all on board had been under the Naval Discipline Act', he writes, with a hint of complacency; 'and as everyone must have been aware that this pleasing state of affairs was a fiction, the men deserve as much credit as the officers, if not more, for the fact that it continued to be observed.'

Despite all this, however, despite even the King's acquiescence, the Admiralty objected to Sir Clements Markham's request that *Discovery* should fly the White Ensign. The Harwich Yacht Club promptly made Scott a member, which enabled him and his ship to sail at least under the Blue Ensign, as well as the club's burgee and the Royal Geographical Society's own swallow-tailed flag. Early in August, *Discovery* arrived at Cowes, where the seas around the Isle of Wight were brightened by the lean and elegant yachts of the rich, the eminent and the aspiring; it was the week of the Royal Regatta. Indeed, *Discovery* found herself almost at once on the wrong side of the social code – she had secured to one of the buoys reserved for the royal yacht. Despite this, however, King Edward and Queen Alexandra came aboard that day; 'it has often been my lot to bid goodbye to an expedition going away on war-like service', said the King. 'It gives me great pleasure to wish goodbye and good luck to an expedition going away on service from which the whole world will benefit.' And there and then he made Scott a member of the Royal Victorian Order, a decoration more personal to the sovereign than almost any other. Thoughtfully, Scott's mother was brought forward to pin the ribbon of the order on his chest.

The next morning, 6 August 1901, *Discovery* cast off and

37

moved decorously past the Needles and out into the English Channel. Sir Clements Markham watching her departure could see at last the hull and spars, the bow, smokestack and blunt stern of his long ambition turned into reality. For him all was optimism, even euphoria, a sturdy welling of confidence in the ship he had sent on its way southward, and in the men who sailed her. Scott, judging from his own words, was more mixed in his feelings; 'Old Mooney' still had his dreams, his melancholy, those strange lapses into an impenetrable introspection upon which all his friends remarked. 'In those days', he tells us, 'we thought much of the grim possibilities of our voyage. There was ever present before us the unpleasant reflection that we might start off with a flourish of trumpets and return with failure.' An untried commander leading untried men into an unknown and forbidding continent – he might well be forgiven thoughts of failure as the coast of southern England slipped further and further into the August haze.

OPPOSITE King Edward VII with Queen Alexandra and Princess Victoria on board the *Discovery* at Cowes just before she sailed for the Antarctic on 5 August 1901. Sir Clements Markham is presenting Captain Scott to his Majesty.

2 Discovery

Nov. 21. 1903.

Mount Erebus, with smoking chimney geysers - from the South.

THE OBJECTS OF THE EXPEDITION are a) to determine, as far as possible, the nature, condition and extent of that portion of the South Polar lands which is included in the scope of your expedition; and b) to make a magnetic survey in the southern regions to the south of the 40th parallel, and to carry on meteorological, oceanographic, geological, biological and physical investigations and researches. Neither of these objects is to be sacrificed to the other.

Thus begin the instructions to Scott, drawn up by a special sub-committee of four, delegates of the thirty-two strong Joint Committee. They set out in detail the kinds of work upon which the committee hoped Scott would be able to engage. They mention again the once vexed question of wintering on the ice. If Scott decided to do so, they suggest, 'your efforts as regards geographical exploration should be ... an advance into the western mountains, an advance to the south, and an exploration of the volcanic regions.' They recognise, however, that 'in an enterprise of this nature much must be left to the discretion and judgement of the commanding officer, and we fully confide in your combined energy and prudence for the successful issue of a voyage which will command the attentions of all persons interested in navigation and science throughout the civilised world.'

The man to whom these instructions were addressed was now thirty-four. He was not tall, being about five feet nine, but he had the broad chest and narrow hips of a man in whose physical condition one could have confidence. He was naturally rather pale, but heavy eyebrows seemed to darken his face. From below them, deep blue eyes looked steadily out at a world they challenged, yet for which they also seemed to express a strange compassion. He had a well-rounded head with strong features, his face rather square, with a firm chin and a brow in which the promise of intelligence was perhaps accentuated by the thinning brown hair above. His expression was stubborn, serious, even solemn, perhaps a little cold and autocratic; only the slightly tip-tilted nose and the occasional brightness in his eyes hinted at any inner frivolity. He could charm and his smile was warm, yet there was often about him a brooding air of solitariness, even of melancholy. His mouth, with its rounded lips, suggests a leaning towards sensuality and pleasure, but he had learned control early; even his temper, always quick, was now almost entirely in harness. Only his dreaming, his strange absent-mindedness, sometimes continued to defeat him. He endeavoured to

PREVIOUS PAGES Mount Erebus drawn by Edward Wilson.

OPPOSITE Sketch of Captain Scott aboard the *Discovery* by Edward Wilson.

42

E.a.W.

Capt. Scott.
Discovery
1901.

give the impression, and perhaps believed it to be the truth, that he was a conventionally energetic naval officer, taken up with the duties and ringed by the opinions permitted to a man of his position; but one senses that behind and within this conventionalised figure, another, far more complex, far more sensitive person lay curbed, perhaps chained, yet only dormant.

Nevertheless, in this matter of Antarctic exploration he had been in some sense almost a puppet. He was not after all in *Discovery* because of some long-considered choice, some ambition conceived in childhood and implacably pursued. Rather he was there as the instrument of Sir Clements Markham's intentions. It was almost exactly fourteen years since Markham, visiting St Kitts, had watched the midshipmen of the Training Squadron race their ships' cutters and written, 'The race tried several qualities. For a long time it was a close thing ... but Scott won the race.' From that moment on he had been the unseen if quiescent director of Scott's destiny, watching and waiting as the young man matured in the set processes of a naval officer's career, biding his time until suddenly in 1899 he had twitched the strings and settled this promising lieutenant into his new and unexpected posture. Now, however, the puppet had as it were outrun Markham's strings; selected, prepared, fussed over and fought for, Scott now had to make the transition into the kind of man Sir Clements had all those years felt confident he would become.

The first problem which faced the expedition was the nature of the vessel they sailed in. 'Great as may be the advantage of having a new ship', Scott wrote, 'it can readily be understood that there are also serious drawbacks.' *Discovery*, built to withstand the pressures of moving polar ice, was slow. As a result the opportunities Scott had hoped for to test and experiment with some of the new equipment never came. 'Some of these devices were new, and with all we were unfamiliar; and the fact that we were unable to practise with them during the outward voyage was severely felt when they came to be used afterwards in the Antarctic regions.' Then it became clear that the ship had sprung a slow but persistent leak. The Dundee builders had insisted, despite the normal experience of wooden ships, that no such leak would occur; 'in consequence of this, no flooring had been placed in the holds to lift the provisions above any water which might collect. ... When the water began to enter, therefore ... it rose amongst the cases, causing a good deal of damage.'

Yet as he wrote to his mother, 'The ship is a magnificent sea boat, smooth and easy in every movement, a positive cradle on the deep.' After rounding the Cape of Good Hope and reaching the 'Roaring Forties', Scott became 'more and more satisfied with the seaworthy qualities of our small ship'. He seemed on the whole equally satisfied with his personnel, although one man was discharged for bad behaviour and another exchanged when it was found he had contracted syphilis. The worst disagreements arose between Scott and George Murray, a noted botanist who had become temporary director of the scientific staff. Due to sail with them to Melbourne, he abruptly and rather huffily departed during their short stay in Cape Town, leaving Scott to deal with the scientific as well as the administrative side of the expedition. Dr H. R. Mill, the Royal Geographical Society's librarian, a frail and elderly man rather courageously sailing with the expedition as far as South Africa, wrote to Scott's mother, 'Captain Scott has shown a power that, I must own, surprised me in mastering the details of all the scientific work which is being arranged.'

In mid November *Discovery* crossed the 60th parallel and shortly afterwards had her first sight of what after all they were sailing round the world to see – ice. Wilson noted in his diary, 'After prayers I was on the bridge with Michael Barne. . . . Suddenly however Michael went mad and rushed down the ladder and shouted "Ice!" down the ward-room skylight. He slipped in his hurry and came a regular howler, but never stopped to pick up. . . . Huge jokes and everyone in the most boisterous spirits and champagne at once ordered for dinner this evening.' That night Scott noted, 'what light remained was reflected in a ghostly glimmer from the white surface of the pack; now and again a white snow petrel flitted through the gloom, the grinding of the floes against the ship's side was mingled with the more subdued hush of their rise and fall on the long swell, and for the first time we felt something of the solemnity of these great southern solitudes.'

At the end of November the expedition arrived at Lyttleton, New Zealand, for the last overhaul, refit and victualling, almost the last contact with the familiar world of men, houses, trees and temperate climate. The New Zealand Government provided an unexpected £1000, the harbour dues were waived,

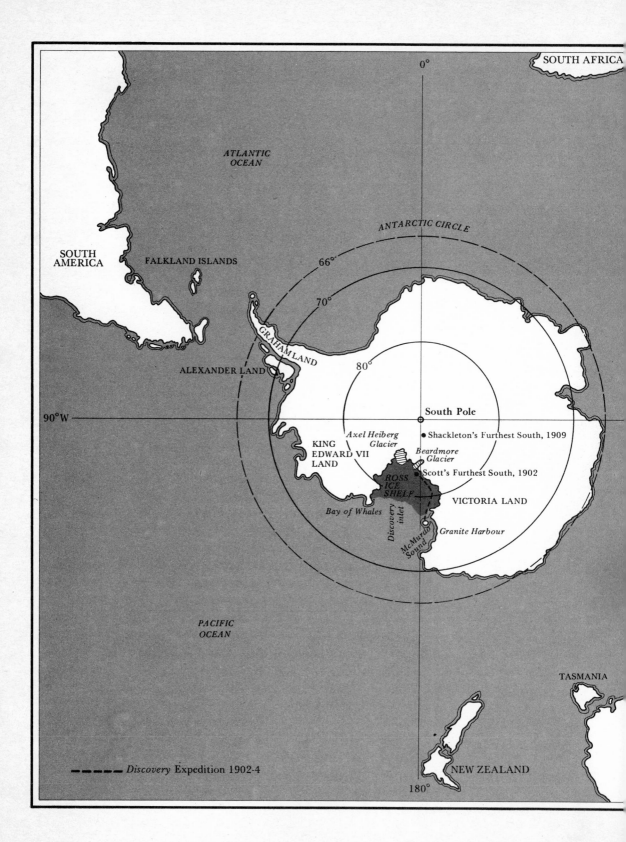

SOUTH AFRICA

ATLANTIC OCEAN

ANTARCTIC CIRCLE

SOUTH AMERICA

FALKLAND ISLANDS

66°

70°

GRAHAM LAND

ALEXANDER LAND

80°

90°W

South Pole

Shackleton's Furthest South, 1909

Axel Heiberg Glacier

KING EDWARD VII LAND

Beardmore Glacier

Scott's Furthest South, 1902

ROSS ICE SHELF

VICTORIA LAND

Bay of Whales

Discovery Inlet

Granite Harbour

McMurdo Sound

PACIFIC OCEAN

TASMANIA

— — — — — *Discovery* Expedition 1902-4

NEW ZEALAND

180°

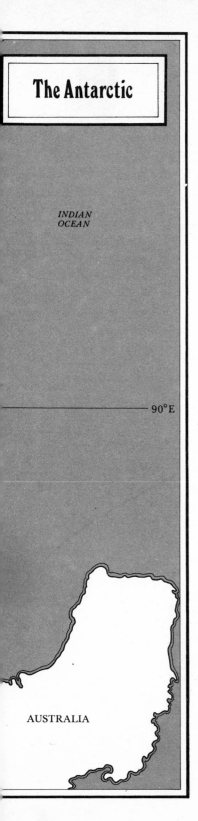

The Antarctic

INDIAN
OCEAN

90°E

AUSTRALIA

travel and accommodation were free, local farmers made a gift of a flock of sheep. Nevertheless, Scott had to apply to London for more money; on 6 December Cocks, the Royal Geographical Society's treasurer, commented on Scott's cable asking for a further £500, 'I suppose we must send it but I do so with regret.' A fortnight later he was even more outraged: 'He wants £400 more!! to cover advances. Under the circumstances, I see nothing for it but to send it and to hope for the best.'

Meanwhile, it had been decided in London to arrange for a relief ship to make its way to *Discovery* at the end of the following year. Scott wrote to the Presidents of the two great Societies, 'It is with great satisfaction I learn it is intended to send a relief ship. . . . I had intended writing most urgently to you on this subject, knowing how absolutely our retreat would otherwise be cut off, should any accident result in the loss of the *Discovery*.'

On 21 December, *Discovery* having been dry-docked, inspected, scraped, caulked and refloated in an effort to dam that famous leak, the expedition left Lyttleton. The ship was heavily laden and sluggish, so much so that Scott wrote that he did not 'look forward with pleasure to crossing the stormiest ocean in the world'. Even the decks were crowded, largely with mutually antipathetic flocks of sheep and dogs.

Yet everywhere was celebration and laudatory farewell. Wilson noted that they 'went out amid immense cheering with steamers crowded with visitors on each side of us and following in our wake', while Scott himself tells us, 'Special trains from Christchurch had borne thousands to the port to wish us farewell. Wharves and quays were packed with enthusiastic figures.' Leading Stoker Lashly, who was to become one of the ablest and steadiest of Scott's team, says in his restrained way, 'We had a splendid send off – all the ships in the harbour came out to the heads and wished us God speed and a safe return. . . .'

Yet in a way one cannot help searching for symbolic value, tragedy instantly checked euphoria. A sailor named Bonner, cheering enthusiastically high on the mainmast, lost his hold and fell to the deck, dying instantly. As Scott describes it, 'sadness and gloom descended on the ship and damped for the time all thought of our future in the South'. A call at Dunedin, a final scratching of farewells to catch the mails to England, then the dirt and labour of coaling; another crowd, more cheers, more trumpeting and hooting from assembled ships; at last out into a freshening north-easterly. 'A hoarse shout and a hoarser whistling from our friendly tug, a final wave from the signal station on the cliff, and we were away.' Thus Scott described the departure and perhaps one is not wrong to catch a certain relief in his tone.

The Antarctic is a region difficult to define, consisting of the sparsely-islanded wastes of the Southern Ocean which centre on the Antarctic continent. This last is a landmass some five and a half million square miles in area; the southern capes of Africa and America seem to stab at it, and Australia heaves towards it like a whale. It is the globe's most remote continent, for the nearest mainland is some 600 miles distant. Almost the whole of it is covered by an ice sheet with an average thickness of 6000 feet. Over ninety per cent of all the snow and ice in the world lies on or around this bleak continent and only the occasional rocky peak thrusts bitterly through its integument. The coldest places on earth are to be found here – on the high plateau, which even below the ice rises to 13,000 feet, temperatures down to $-124\,°F$ have been recorded. Around the Pole itself, the annual mean temperature is somewhere around $-65\,°F$, cold enough to turn kerosene to jelly. Local meteorological conditions often produce hurricanes; although there is a low precipitation rate, these whip up the fine, granular snow into blizzards which are more like the sandstorms of the Sahara. Once such strong winds set in they tend to persist – the continent's single great hazard to man. For it is not only the temperature level but wind-chill which determines how cold a man will feel; nipping and clawing at the exposed parts of the body – the hands, the face – it is this which will cause frost-bite and, if prolonged, the general lethargy which is the prelude to death in these regions of the earth. It is no wonder that most of this continent is almost entirely desert; only a few lichens and mosses grow there. As a result there are no land animals and thus no men who, like the Eskimos of the north, have learned how to adapt themselves to the conditions. The largest land creature is *Belgica antarctica* – the local midge. On the other hand, the sea is rich in animal and vegetable life, able to support seals, whales, and several varieties of birds, most notably those sociable, curious and arrogant creatures the penguins.

At the same time as the hazards of wind and ice may harass the traveller, so the curious optical effects of Antarctica may confuse him. In the total absence of dust and haze, visibility is

48

extraordinary – mountains have been sighted at a distance of nearly 300 miles. Objects which seem only a few miles distant turn out to be twenty or thirty miles away, an effect heightened by the absence of any vegetation which might otherwise give back to man his sense of scale. Refraction of light (due to temperature inversion when the upper air is warmer than the lower) causes mirages, while the millions of tiny ice crystals which float high in the atmosphere produce refraction phenomena which blaze and glitter in the pale, unclouded sky; arcs of light, false suns and moons, or the real sun and moon haloed by bands of unearthly brightness. And then at night – that long night of the polar world – the *aurora australis* burns and glows in great bands

Huge, towering icebergs, glittering islands sometimes several miles square, are a feature of the southern continent.

Emperor Penguins
April 17. 1902.

...eror Penguins
April. 17. 1902.

RIGHT Leopard seals drawn by Wilson for the May 1902 edition of *The South Polar Times*. There are no animals in the bleak Antarctic wastes, but the seas are turbulent with life, supporting seals, several kinds of whales and a variety of birds.

BELOW Mount Erebus by Edward Wilson.

of green and white, flying shafts of light, shining curtains of an ethereal luminosity, the vast grandeur of a red and purple brightness rippling up the sky like fire.

Towards this region of great rigour, hallucination, heavenly portents and utter loneliness, Scott and his small party were now making their slow but determined way. On 2 January 1902, Wilson was writing, 'Soon after lunch when Royds was on watch, he sighted our first ice, a fair sized berg . . .' and on the following day *Discovery* crossed the Antarctic Circle, those sailing in her, as Scott wrote, 'little thinking how long a time would elapse before we recrossed it'. Yet he was not displeased; as he put it in his book, 'the struggles and trials of preparation and the anxiety of delays were over, and the haste of our long voyage was forgotten in the fact that we had reached the field of our labours. . . .'

The next stage in their progress south was the ship's entry into pack ice; 'for several days we were destined to force our way through the grinding floes, making for the open pools, and taking advantage of every favourable lead when the ice loosened'. They chose 5 January, perhaps because it was a Sunday, to celebrate the Christmas they had missed in their departure from New Zealand; secured to an ice floe, Scott had members of the expedition make their first experiments with snow shoes and skis. Thus progressing and learning, they watched the ice pack pass by, saw once again open water about them: 'the shout of "Land in sight" . . . only added to an already joyful frame of mind', Scott recalled.

On 9 January Wilson recorded, 'a day to be remembered, for we landed on the Antarctic continent, at Cape Adare . . . .', the point at which Borchgrevink's *Southern Cross* party had landed only a few years before. The hut those first explorers had used during their long winter still stood and Bernacchi, who had been one of them and was now physicist with Scott, guided these new visitors around the bunks and debris of the earlier expedition. Scott, with his inner melancholy, noted, 'There is always something sad in contemplating the deserted dwellings of mankind.' The thought of Hanson, the naturalist with the *Southern Cross* party who had died and been buried at Cape Adare, moved him to write, 'So there rest the remains of the only human being who has found burial on this great Southern Continent, and above his body still stands, in touching memorial, a plain wooden cross.' The tone is indicative of

Cape Adare, where the expedition first set foot on the Antarctic continent on 9 January 1902. The hut in the background was built by Borchgrevink's party. Drawing by Edward Wilson.

Cape Adare & the Southern Cross Hut.

Jan. 19. 1902.   75° 32′ S. 164° 52′ E   Pans of New Ice.

Pans of new ice; Edward Wilson.

something brooding in Scott. Wilson in his diary put it differently: 'We ... began to hunt for Nicolai Hanson's grave, which was marked by a big stone and an iron cross. But nowhere could we find it. . . . Bernacchi was so anxious to see that Hanson's grave was all right that after dinner he started up and found it all safe, and with Barne and Koettlitz brought home a number of skua fledglings. . . .' The approach is different, perhaps as becomes a medical man and a scientist; yet in retrospect Scott makes a strange naval officer, with his inner sadness and his bouts of absent-mindedness.

On 10 January *Discovery* weighed anchor and moved on southward. Almost immediately caught in a strong and unexpected tidal current which seemed about to sweep gigantic ice floes over their ship and themselves to destruction, Scott and the officers of the watch – most notably the first lieutenant, Armitage, who was conning the ship from aloft – appear to have kept admirably calm; yet when they were safe Scott felt a lesson had been learned: 'We were here to fight the elements with their icy weapons, and once and for all this taught me not to undervalue the enemy.'

A gale sent them for shelter under the bulk of Coulman Island:

54

'the engines were eased when we were nearly two miles from the cliffs, under the impression that they were only a few hundred yards away.' In a sea littered with small icebergs and in a wind of nearly 100 miles an hour, *Discovery* spent an uncomfortable and dangerous night. By the following evening, however, she lay in some security in an inlet off Lady Newnes Bay (loyally named after their sponsor's wife by the men of the *Southern Cross* expedition) and members of her crew were at work on the ice: 'not a pleasant task, but one we regarded as very necessary – namely, that of adding to our larder sundry joints of seal. ... It seemed a terrible desecration to come to this quiet spot only to murder its innocent inhabitants. . . .'

As they travelled farther south and the days of January passed, Scott points out, 'We were now in a latitude where it was most desirable that we should make a diligent search for safe winter quarters for the ship.' Wood Bay, which in England had been considered as a base, had already been left behind, discarded because of the difficulties of sledging southwards from it. An inlet, named Granite Harbour, seemed to offer shelter and secure anchorage, and Scott left it 'satisfied that we had discovered a place which would serve us for wintering in default of a better'. A day later *Discovery* was pushing into McMurdo Sound and Scott was writing in his diary that 'so far as the eye can see there must be a plain stretching directly to the south. ... We now see that if fortune allows us to winter in either of the two harbours we have found, we shall have good prospect of getting to the south. . . .'

They now swung eastward, to examine the length and solidity of the Great Ice Barrier (as Ross had called it when stopped in his southward, sea-borne progress over half a century before; today it is called the Ross Ice Shelf in his memory). On 22 January a whaleboat set out, 'somewhat crowded with sixteen persons and a number of magnetic instruments' and landed on the rocky shores of Cape Crozier. With Lieutenant Royds, Scott and Wilson climbed a nearby volcanic peak, from which, says Scott, 'we were rewarded by a first view of the Great Ice Barrier ... the barrier edge, in shadow, looked like a long narrowing black ribbon as it ran with slight windings to the eastern horizon. South of this line ... a vast plain extended indefinitely ... further yet to the south the sun faced us, and the plain was lost in the glitter of its reflection.' For several days *Discovery* sailed eastwards with the rise and fall of the great ice cliffs always to starboard. It was a largely monotonous sight, although sometimes relieved by faults and cavities in the cliff face; Wilson noted on 28 January, 'In these cliffs were the most wonderful bright blue caves, and the whole face was hung with long thin icicles, which made the most fascinating grottos with the pure blue depths of the caves and cracks.'

On 29 January Scott reached and passed the farthest point Ross had achieved, a position from which he had reported seeing land to the south-east. Alas, Scott's crew 'alike from below and from aloft ... could see nothing, and were obliged to conclude that the report was based on one of those strange optical illusions which are so common in this region. ...' The next day, however, they came at last to the end of the ice shelf and saw rock again, exposed to the keen Antarctic air. They had found new territory, perhaps the edge of that which Ross had seen from farther off; Scott named it King Edward VII Land. After a day spent in slightly aimless manœuvrings during which Scott and Armitage confessed themselves lost, *Discovery* once more approached this coastline. The outline of the nearest range of hills, Scott wrote, 'suggested a volcanic country' – 'the high land extended far back beyond the coastal hills ... our new-found land was ... a country of considerable altitude and extent.'

Yet his party had neither the time nor the experience to explore it, and it was a little regretfully that Scott turned west once more and headed towards McMurdo Sound. On 4 February, however, he decided that the time had come to try out one item of modern equipment which they were the first to use in polar regions: a balloon. While Armitage led a small sledging party away to the south, the envelope was placed on the snow and slowly inflated. Leading Stoker Lashly tells us that a troublesome wind 'died away at 8 o'clock and we prepared the balloon for inflating. It was rather a cold job. ... However, we got through it very well, and in pretty good time after tearing the balloon twice and mending the same. Captain Scott made his first ascent up to about 700 feet.'

Scott himself was rather less phlegmatic. It was the first and the only aeronautical adventure of his life and

... as I swayed about in what appeared a very inadequate basket and gazed down on the rapidly diminishing figures below I felt some doubt as to whether I had been wise in my choice. ... I heard the word 'sand' borne up from below and remembered the bags at my feet ... with thoughtless inexperience I seized them wholesale and flung them out,

The famous balloon experiment was abandoned
after Scott's rather hair-raising ascent. This photograph
shows the balloon with the *Discovery* in the
background; the ship's larder of seal meat can be
be seen in the rigging.

McCormick's Skua.

april · 1902 ·

Sketches by Edward Wilson
of penguins and (above) of
brown skuas, one of several
species of marine birds
which breed in the
Antarctic, attracted by the
rich supply of fish in the
Southern Ocean.

with the result that 'Eva' shot up suddenly and as the rope tightened commenced to oscillate in a manner that was not at all pleasing.

However, the ascent proved informative, for he discovered that 'the plain continued in a series of long undulations running approximately east to west'. Shackleton was sent up with a camera; then the combination of an increasing wind and a faulty valve brought the operation to an end, not only for that day, but for the rest of the expedition. As Wilson rather sourly commented, 'The whole ballooning business seems to me to be an exceedingly dangerous amusement in the hands of such inexperienced novices as we have on board ... if some of these experts don't come to grief over it out here, it will only be because God has pity on the foolish.' This seems to be the view which finally prevailed.

Armitage returned with more detailed reports about the plain Scott had surveyed from on high, and with notes on their experiences of spending a night in the open. One or two of the men, Scott writes, 'reported most unfavourably on the snoring capabilities of the others'. On 8 February *Discovery* was once again in McMurdo Sound, and work began on erecting the hut which was to give the location its famous name: Hut Point. As temperatures dropped the ship would be frozen-in, providing secure winter quarters. By 14 February Scott could write, 'We have landed all the dogs, and their kennels are ranged over the hillside below the huts', but he complains, 'It is surprising what a number of things have to be done, and what an unconscionable time it takes to do them. The hut-building is slow work, and much of our time has been taken in securing the ship. ... Much work is before us when the huts are up.' However, all of them laboured happily at learning to ski, and when on 16 February 'our football and general athletic ground broke away ... skiing became a still more popular amusement.'

More difficult than skiing, however, and less fun, was learning to control the dog teams. Without any experience in this art, which Nansen had devoted much time to learning, the British explorers found that again and again their clumsiness turned an apparently disciplined team into a chaos of yelping, snarling, snapping fur. Unaware of the pack instincts of their dogs, they changed animals from one team to another, only to find that the interloper would be almost – at times actually – torn to pieces by the others. Then there were accidents – the steward, Ford,

Cramped conditions inside
the tent; drawing by
Edward Wilson.

broke a leg, Royds fell overboard but managed to scramble
back to safety, Scott himself wrenched a knee on the ski slopes.

Because of this last mishap it was Royds who led out a sledge
party carrying details of their winter quarters to be added to the
cache already left at Cape Crozier for the expected relief ship.
As a result, 11 March 'was to be one of our blackest days in the
Antarctic'. Slowed down by the conditions, only Royds and a
handful of men thrust on to Cape Crozier, leaving the rest of the
party to return to *Discovery* under Lieutenant Barne. Caught by
a blizzard as they crossed an ice slope, this group lost contact
with one of its members, a young steward named Hare. As they

turned to look for him, Petty Officer Evans who was long to be one of Scott's stalwarts, lost his footing and slid away down the slope. Barne, searching for him, slid after him, as did Leading Stoker Quartley a little later. The remaining five waited for a while, then turned to make their way towards where they hoped *Discovery* lay. Suddenly they found themselves on a steep slope, the sea 500 feet below, abruptly visible, grey, ice-spattered. All pulled back but Vince, in fur boots which gave him no purchase, could not stop himself. In a moment he had gone, plunging down the slope and out of sight into the water. When the remaining four finally climbed over the side of the ship, they were half frozen and in a state of shock. Vince was almost certainly dead, Hare and the other three missing. Armitage was at once ordered away with a search party but Scott showed his inner suffering when he wrote: 'Hatefully conscious of my inability to help on account of my injured leg, my own mind seemed barren of all suggestions of further help which we might render.'

However, steam was raised in order that the siren could be sounded. Shackleton took a whaler out on a forlorn search of the ice floes, and then, out of the grey of the drifting snow, the geologist, Ferrar, appeared followed by Evans, Barne and Quartley. Able Seaman Wild, over and over again a hero, who had led the earlier survivors back to *Discovery* and then gone out again to guide Armitage, had brought the rescuers to the sledges which the party had abandoned; nearby they had found the three missing men. Of Hare, however, there was no sign. The next day search parties were out again, but by the evening Wilson was writing, 'All hope of saving Vince or Hare was now given up.' But the day following Scott put jubilantly in his diary, 'A very extraordinary thing has happened. At 10 am a figure was seen descending the hillside. . . . In a minute or two we recognised the figure as that of young Hare, and in less than five he was aboard.' Miraculously, the young man, whom Wilson had described as 'a by no means robust boy of 21', had survived forty-eight hours in the open, without shelter, during a period of exceptional wind and snow. It was, in fact, snow which had probably saved him, for he had slept and been covered over, perhaps for thirty-six hours. Once back in the ship, however, Scott (who differs from Wilson in saying the boy was only eighteen) tells us, 'He went placidly off to sleep whilst objecting to the inadequacy of a milk diet.'

Perhaps no one has ever
conveyed the spare beauty of
the Antarctic, the dazzling
tricks of its light, the
vastness and majesty of its
storm-riven surface, better
than Edward Wilson, for
whom, as artist to the Scott
expeditions, they provided
an endless source of
inspiration.

ABOVE Earth shadows.
The atmosphere of the
Antarctic produced fantastic
shapes and colours, brilliant
mirages and unsettling
distortions of distance.
ABOVE RIGHT View across
McMurdo Sound.
RIGHT Cape Wadworth,
Coulman Island to Lady
Newnes Bay.

Seal skins being salted for
preservation purposes.

That the whole party was always potentially in danger was
emphasised when in May the boatswain and the second
engineer, thinking the peninsula beside which *Discovery* was
anchored was an island, tried to walk around it and by following
the shore only succeeded in getting further and further away.
'There must be no more of this casual walking about', wrote
Scott. But one did not need to be elaborately careless to put oneself in jeopardy; on 4 August Bernacchi and Skelton, the
engineer, lost their way in the two hundred yards between the
hut ashore and the ship. For nearly two hours they wandered in
circles, while the rising blizzard flung snow mountainously at
them and they shouted unsuccessfully for help. Only the arrival
of a second party under Royds, also returning to the ship,
prevented a disaster almost ludicrous in its location – both men
were badly frost-bitten and as Scott relates, 'In the nick of time
they were rescued within thirty yards of their goal, but without
any knowledge of the fact.'

By now *Discovery* was deep into the polar night. The men

64

worked hard, preparing for the voyages planned for the spring, and they kept themselves amused by entertainments at the 'Royal Terror Theatre', and by the publication of *The South Polar Times*, a periodical edited by Shackleton, illustrated by Wilson and written by everyone who could put pen to paper; Scott contributed articles and a regular acrostic. By September the first of the longer sledge journeys was beginning. Scott himself made a ninety-mile journey, laying depots for that long dash southward which was in the end the main reason he had come all this way. His party was caught in a blizzard and forced to return to the ship, before setting out again later in the month. In October there was an outbreak of scurvy which Scott attributed to the tinned meat they were eating (forced to do so in part by his own soft-hearted reluctance to order the killing of

Petty Officers Evans and Crean mending sleeping bags.

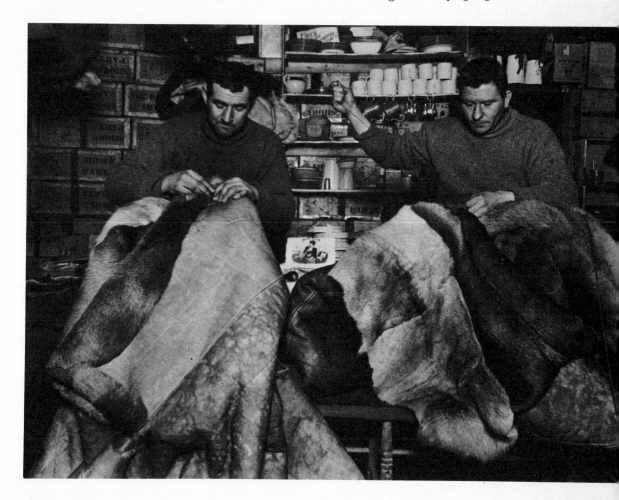

seals). Fresh meat was hunted, Dr Koettlitz grew crops of mustard and cress and slowly the outbreak subsided – but as Wilson wrote at the time, 'now we know what to expect from the sledging work this summer'.

Their attention was now turning more and more to sledging; despite the hard work and the setbacks, there was a sense among all of them that the climax of the expedition was approaching. Scott and his companions were to be launched to the south as the final party of a climbing expedition might be launched towards the summit of some Himalyan giant, everyone realising that in that concentrated effort all of them would find their vindication and reward.

On 12 June Wilson had written that

... the Skipper told me he had taken the long journey towards the South Pole for himself, and had decided that to get a long way south the party must be a small one ... he hadn't decided whether two men was best or three, but in any case would I go with him? My surprise can be guessed. ... I then argued for three men rather than two. The weights are not proportionately increased ... yet there is an extra man to work at the job. Then if one gets ill, all *could* get back if there were three. .... 'Who then was to be the third?' he said. So I told him it wasn't for me to suggest anyone. He then said, he need hardly have asked me because he knew who I would say, and added that he was the man he would have chosen himself. So then I knew it was Shackleton. ....

Wilson the friend, Shackleton the rival; here for the supreme moment of the expedition Scott's judgement caused him to overrule his previous insistence on a team chosen almost entirely from the Navy and to pick Shackleton, an officer from the Merchant Marine. Scott gives no reasons for picking 'Shackle' but in many ways he was an obvious choice; good-humoured, energetic, strong, and at this time a great friend of Wilson. It may even be that Scott wished to set out with a man against whom he could measure himself.

On 30 October, the supporting party under Barne set off southwards. One sledge bore the legend, 'No Dogs Need Apply'; all the available teams were being kept for the main thrust. Last letters were written; champagne was drunk in the wardroom. On 2 November, Wilson wrote, 'At last we started, though it was a cold and windy day.' Scott, even more drily, put, 'We are off at last', but went on to describe the scene –

OPPOSITE Edward Wilson working on one of his sketches.

'every soul was gathered on the floe to bid us farewell ... away we went admist the wild cheers of our comrades.'

They made good progress. By the end of the first day they had caught up Barne's party and for the next few days first one then the other team led. But blizzards caught them, holding them immobile in their tents. The dogs too were often a problem – badly chosen, badly handled, of the wrong breed, they were probably more trouble than they were worth.

On 15 November Barne, with the last of the supporting party, turned back towards McMurdo Sound. Scott wrote, 'Confident in ourselves, confident in our equipment, and confident in our dog team, we can but feel elated with the prospect that is before us.' Rather more prosaically, Wilson was 'glad to have dropped the other parties, so that now we can shove along as fast as we can'. But, as if in warning, on that first lonely day they travelled only three miles. The dogs were beginning to flag. The next morning the overloaded sledges proved too heavy for the teams to move, and the three men began the labour of relaying the loads – taking half forward, then coming back for the second half – three miles travelled for every mile gained to the south. From the beginning of December, the dogs began to die; cut up and fed to the rest, they provided a little new energy for the survivors. All the same, the party were only averaging around four miles a day and it was already clear that they were not making the speed which would bring them to the Pole.

By now they made a strange spectacle, men and dogs hauling indiscriminately, while the weaker animals lay with glazed eyes upon the sledges. All struggled in soft snow, deep and made for drudgery. For days the sun shone straight into their faces, the light stabbing off the icy surface, the temperature rising until, at around freezing, everyone paradoxically suffered from the heat. In the still air the weight of the silence around them sometimes seemed oppressive; their cries and shouts as they bullied and cajoled their dog teams seemed to float, fade and die in such an unmagnanimous immensity. Sometimes that stillness was broken by an explosive crack, by a fusillade, as the ice responded to its own weight and pressure. Sometimes the tricks light played – the ringed or the repeated sun, the glowing clouds, the floating rainbow-hued circles – made them feel as though they had stumbled into dreams. Food was both short and monotonous; the three men began to dream great meals at night – Wilson records 'splendid foods, ball suppers, sirloins of

OPPOSITE Ernest Henry Shackleton whose outgoing, dashing personality contrasted markedly with the self-disciplined Scott, and who was to become Scott's greatest rival in Antarctic exploration.

beef, caldrons full of steaming vegetables. But one spends all one's time shouting at waiters who won't bring one a plate of anything. . . .'

Ahead of them new land beckoned – 'mountain ranges with splendid peaks . . . here and there rocky precipices . . . stood out bold and dark', as Wilson described it – glittering in the sun or blue against the pale sky, then abruptly obscured by the grey whiplash of a blizzard. This they knew was the mainland of the continent; they were still struggling towards it across its frozen skirt of floating ice. And all the time they suffered the frustrations of their to-and-fro, pendulum progress. On 10 December Scott notes, 'Yesterday we covered only two miles. . . . Snatcher died yesterday; others are getting feeble – it is terrible to see them. The coast cannot be more than ten or twelve miles, but shall we ever reach it? and in what state shall we be to go on?'

On 14 and 15 December they set up depots for their return journey, thus lightening their loads. With enough provisions for four weeks, they now moved on towards the beckoning mountains. A chasm in the ice held them up; with rearranged loads, they moved forward through the long afternoon of 16 December: 'I scarcely know how to describe the blessed relief it is to be free from our relay work. For one-and-thirty awful days we have been at it. . . . It seems now like a nightmare, which grew more and more terrible towards its end.' By 19 December after some reflections on his good fortune in face of the hunger all of them were suffering to be a pipe smoker – 'I have a theory that I am saved some of the worst pangs by my pipe' – Scott noted, 'We are now about ten miles from the land . . . it is a fine scene of a lofty snow-cap, whose smooth rounded outline is broken by the sharper bared peaks, or by the steep disturbing fall of some valley.'

On 21 December Wilson told Scott that he had detected signs of incipient scurvy in Shackleton's gums; grimly, Scott writes, 'Certainly this is a black night, but things must look blacker yet before we decide to turn.' By Christmas Eve Scott was showing signs of the disease; nevertheless, in a mood of some bravado, they celebrated Christmas by travelling a full ten miles and then, as Shackleton's entry makes plain – 'boiled plum pudding and made cocoa' – by more traditional means. He had carried the pudding secretly in the toe of a spare sock – complete with a sprig of artificial holly: 'we have a sense of comfort we have not known for many a day', wrote Scott.

Shackleton, Scott and Wilson (left to right) celebrating Christmas Day, 1902, in latitude 81.45°s. The flags bear the individual coats-of-arms of the three officers, combined with the Union Jack.

The next day Wilson, who had been suffering from snow-blindness in his left eye, began to suffer in his right; by the following day, he was blind. 'The Captain and Shackle did everything for me. Nothing could have been nicer than the way I was treated.' By the end of the year, however, he had recovered and was sketching again, risking frost-bite as always as he bent over his pad.

On 28 December Scott wrote, 'Sights today put us well over the 82nd parallel. We have almost shot our bolt.' Intending to push on by ski the next day the three men instead found themselves confined to their tent by a blizzard. On 31 December they tried at least to reach bare rock and take specimens for the geologists from this bleak and hitherto undiscovered land. But an impassable crevasse finally stopped them; Shackleton photographed the scene; Scott standing among the tumbled peaks and crests of ice, a small, almost pensive figure dark in a world of lunar highlights and abrupt shadows, facing the crumpled, thrusting cliff that bars his progress to the south. They had come to the end of their outward journey – 'if this compares poorly with our hopes and expectations on leaving the ship', Scott wrote, 'it is a more favourable result than we anticipated when those hopes were first blighted by the failure of the dog teams.'

Now turning their backs on the still distant mountains and the coastline they were never able to reach, they began the long, wearisome and dangerous run back to *Discovery*. One by one more dogs died, each fatality exciting Scott's compassion: 'Yesterday, poor little Nell fell on the march, tried to rise, and fell again. . . . Gus fell, quite played out, and just before our halt, to our greater grief, Kid caved in.' They stepped a mast on each sledge and sailed across the ice, the dogs following or, if very weak, riding. By 10 January Shackleton was giving Scott cause for concern – 'I am not feeling happy about his condition' – and the next day he wrote that with 'nothing about one but the unchanging grey it is impossible to avoid a sense of being lost.' Snow was driving at their backs obscuring all landmarks and there was a good chance that they would miss the depots they had laid down on the outward journey. But on 13 January the sun shone fitfully through clouds and in trying to take a sighting Scott almost by accident saw the depot, black on the distant horizon. 'I sprang up and shouted, "Boys, there's the depot". We are not a demonstrative party, but I think we excused ourselves for the wild cheer that greeted this announcement.'

They then had 130 miles to cover to reach the next depot. Shackleton was really ill by now and spitting blood; both Scott and Wilson were affected. All three had let their beards grow, they were black with dirt and sunburn, their clothes were like bundled rags: 'in fact our general appearance and tattered clothing have been a source of some amusement to us of late.' The last two dogs were killed, 'the finale to a tale of tragedy; I scarcely like to write of it'. Scott, who took the responsibility of setting their course, often found it very difficult to do so, particularly when fog, clouds and snow made the sun invisible. On 18 January Shackleton 'gave out. He had a bad attack of

Black Island.

breathlessness ... tonight matters are serious with him again.'
By the 21st, Shackleton seemed better, 'but takes his breakdown
much to heart'.

Shackleton himself says little about his sufferings. His diary
remains cheerful and apparently optimistic; he expects that
their journey will end well. There is no doubt that he did feel
his breakdown very deeply; his pride in his physical being, the
pride of a big man who had always been strong, had been
deeply hurt. But Wilson considered him to be in a most
dangerous condition, and it was clear that scurvy was affecting
him even more seriously than his companions. The fact that he
was a bigger man may have meant that he felt the lack of food
more. In any event, by giving up all man-hauling and allowing
Scott and Wilson to make and break camp, he managed pain-
fully to keep moving; only occasionally did his companions
have to carry him on the sledge.

On 27 January they came in sight of what had become over
the earlier months familiar landmarks. 'Erebus raised its head
above the Bluff range; Terror opened out to the east. ...' The
next day, although Shackleton was coughing again, it was he
who spotted the depot's marker flag. 'At length and at last we
have reached the land of plenty', Scott joyfully recorded.
Nevertheless, Shackleton was still very ill; on 30 January
Wilson wrote, 'Our main object now is to get Shackleton back
to the ship before we get caught in another blizzard.'

Now they were travelling in fine weather but finding the
cracks and crevasses in the ice a constant danger. Wilson
records that he fell eight times on 2 February; Scott writes of
him that he 'has suffered from lameness for many a day; the
cause was plain and we knew it must increase'. It was as well
that the next day Lashly, in *Discovery*, could write laconically

Edward Wilson's panoramic
sketch of the coastline
from the Ross Sea with
Mount Discovery right of
centre.

Mt Discovery   Brown Island.

in his diary, 'Captain sighted about 10 miles off tonight.'

Thankfully Scott and his two companions came aboard the following day. In a lyrical paragraph, he lists the comforts to which they were at last able to surrender: the welcomes, the baths, the gossip, the food – 'a feast which realised the glories of our day-dreams' – and finally the deep sleep in their own bunks, clean sheets about them, the ravening Antarctic safely shut away. They had been travelling for ninety-three days and had covered almost a thousand of the most difficult, the most bizarre, the loneliest miles on earth. They had reached latitude 82°17′s, nearer the South Pole than any man before them. But they had not arrived at it; Scott derived comfort from knowing that 'at least ... we had striven and endured with all our might'.

In the English summer of 1902 a new subscription, headed by the King's £100, had made it possible for Sir Clements Markham to go to Norway and buy a barque-rigged whaler. Renamed *Morning*, she had sailed from London early in July; on 23 January her crew had sighted the masts of *Discovery*, having almost given up the search for her when the red-painted canister left at Cape Crozier had led them on to McMurdo Sound. Thus when Scott came back a few days later, he found that his relief ship had arrived at the ice edge; her captain, a Merchant Marine chief officer named Colbeck, walked the ten miles between the ships to speak to Scott on the night of his homecoming. It was another fortnight before Scott was strong enough to return the visit.

The other exploratory parties which had been planned for that season had done their work without too appalling an adventure to darken the achievements of any of them. Armitage had made a 52-day journey driving west into Victoria Land, climbing at one point to nearly 10,000 feet, then returning with one man in the party in a state of collapse. On one march Armitage had fallen into a crevasse, being saved by luck, Lieutenant Skelton and the ropes; nevertheless he could claim that he had led men to the inland ice cap, the first to tramp and struggle across its slopes. Another party under Royds had made the journey to Cape Crozier, to take a further look at that area's huge colonies of Emperor and Adélie penguins. The previous October Skelton had first examined the former's nesting ground, a discovery of which Scott had written, 'He ... wondered if at last the breeding place of these mysterious birds had been discovered – it seemed almost too good to be true.' Thereafter the work done in recording the habits of this penguin, 'the truest type of our region', was not the least important of the expedition's research.

On Scott's orders *Discovery* had been made ready for sea. But the ice had locked her in place and as time passed it became clear that it would not let her go. Colbeck had brought from the Joint Committee the instruction that Scott should 'extricate yourself from your winter quarters with as little loss of time as possible'. However, despite all efforts and all hopes, *Discovery* gave no sign that she was about to budge; and Scott seems at no point to have had the intention of abandoning her. On 8 February, Lashly wrote in his matter-of-fact way, 'One year today we arrived here and there is no sign of the ice breaking yet. It is quite possible we may have to winter here again, although there is time yet.' Time, however, brought no relief – if relief it would have been for these men now so committed to their loneliness. *Morning* prepared to sail away again; the long night was once more on its way. Scott decided that for this second winter he needed fewer men and asked for volunteers to return to Britain. 'The result is curiously satisfactory. There are eight names on the list, and not only that, but these names are precisely those which I should have placed there ... we shall be left with the pick of our company, all on good terms. . . .' There was for a while some question of Armitage, the second-in-command, returning home, Armitage believing that Scott resented his Merchant Service status and feeling some strain and friction between them, while Scott was of the opinion that Armitage ought to return for the sake of his wife and his marriage.

Shackleton on the other hand did return, on medical grounds, for after his serious illness Scott felt that physically he could be a danger both to himself and the expedition. He went unwillingly; as *Morning* left he stood weeping on the deck. Wilson who knew that the decision 'had upset him a great deal as he was very keen indeed to stop and see the thing through' nevertheless added, 'It is certainly wiser for him to go home though.' Sub-Lieutenant Mulock, Royal Navy, took his place. The men who were sent home were, like Shackle, from the Merchant Marine. It is no wonder that the idea should have taken hold that Scott had used *Morning*'s visit to increase among his party the representation of his own beloved Service. Indeed, for the second winter, he had an almost entirely naval team. In later years,

The Illustrated London News ran special features on Scott's expedition, written by Shackleton, which were received with great excitement by an eager and responsive public.
ABOVE One of the publicity announcements.
OPPOSITE Lieutenant Armitage's narrow escape from a crevasse.

EAW.

A Barnitap.
"Dreaming"
1901.

Armitage certainly began stating quite bluntly that this had been Scott's intention, and that his sending away of Shackleton had been the result of a personal feeling rather than any concern for the big man's health. No one knows now what passed between Scott and Shackle on their desperate journey. In public, despite later disputes, they were always moderately polite to each other, giving each other credit for courage and honour. Yet one always senses the rivalry, the unspoken objections, the subconscious rancour. Perhaps the two men were incompatible, opposites, each a reversed version of the other; Scott outwardly cool, melancholy, controlled, a little shy, given to periods of abstraction, yet inwardly a romantic, a taker-up of forlorn hopes, a joyful sufferer; Shackleton breezy, extrovert, aware of fame, happy to make a good impression, an adventurer, a rolling stone, an exaggerator of his feats and feelings. It is likely that two such men will be uneasy with each other, suspicious, locked in a mutual miscomprehension which, in close proximity or over the years, may harden to antipathy.

On 2 March *Morning* sailed, Shackleton and the rest aboard, to take first news of the expedition to a world made slightly nervous by the long silence. Radio and news film brought no instant information in those days; men wandered into the vastnesses of Pole or jungle, the ice or the underbrush closed behind them, they vanished from view – sometimes for ever, sometimes for a year, or two, or three, before emerging to the plaudits of an astonished world. Yet the news of Scott, when it did arrive, renewed dissension between the two august Societies which had sponsored him: why had Scott disregarded his instructions and chosen to winter where he was instead of coming home? Markham rallied the Royal Geographical Society – it recorded 'its full approval of Capt. Scott's proceedings and its confidence in his judgement'. On the whole the admiring world endorsed this view; in May Scott's mother wrote to him, 'I have had congratulations on all sides and from all parts of Europe. . . . All the Polar men are so full of it, they alone understand the difficulties.' Unfortunately the government took a cooler view; asked for £12,000 spread over two years they refused to help any more. Balfour implied that the Joint Committee had been less open than it should have been about what the expedition would cost; confidence, he said, had been rudely shaken. The Royal Society continued doubtful of its part in the venture.

OPPOSITE Sketch by Edward Wilson of Lieutenant Armitage relaxing aboard the *Discovery*.

Max Beerbohm's cartoon of the Prime Minister, Arthur Balfour.

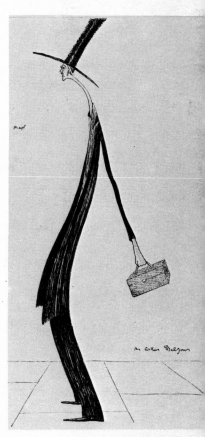

Then the Treasury shifted ground – they would spend money on a relief expedition, provided *Morning* were handed over to the Admiralty. Markham, coerced, signed over the ship, losing in the process £800 which to his anguish the government refused to refund; the Admiralty announced that whoever else stayed on the ice during the next relief visit, the naval men would not: it added that 'if the *Discovery* cannot be freed from the ice in time ... she is to be abandoned'. In this way did the politicians and administrators support a venture which later they were happy to claim as British, as in some sense enhancing the reputation and the honour due to them as countrymen of Scott, as governors of the land he came from.

Scott himself was preparing for the sledging season to come. He walked, climbing the slopes, watching the northern horizon as it lightened, a distant red and gold signalling the slow return of the sun. 'I am not sure that a polar night is not worth the living through for the mere joy of seeing the day come back', he wrote. And, towards the end of August, as 'the rim of the re-fracted sun could just be seen above the northern horizon', he states, 'Life in these regions has lost any terror it ever possessed for us.' By 6 September he was able to write, 'Tomorrow we start our sledging. . . . The ship is in a state of bustle, people flying to and fro. . . . To judge by the laughter and excitement we might be boys escaping from school.'

Royds and Wilson set off for Cape Crozier and the penguins; Barne and Mulock began laying depots for the journey they were to make to the south; Scott himself travelled westward, to lay depots for the journey he was intending to make in the direction Armitage had taken the year before. By early October he was ready; on 12 October he set out. He made good progress, but the moraine on the Ferrar Glacier began to tear at the metal on the runners of his party's four sledges. Three of the four became almost useless – 'the German silver was split to ribbons and the wood deeply scored' – and they had to turn back. The next day, 19 October, 'we came as near flying as is possible with a sledge party'; they made twenty-seven miles, twenty-four the day after, and by 22 October were back on board *Discovery*. Four days later they set out again; Lashly, who was one of the party, wrote, 'Hope we shall have better luck with the sledges this time.'

But the sledges continued giving trouble on the hard glacier ice. When they reached the depot laid the month before, they

found the lid of the instrument box had been blown away and with it, *Hints to Travellers*, a booklet issued by the Royal Geographical Society which gave data navigators need in order to take accurate sights. Scott, however, was reluctant to turn back again and with the agreement of his companions decided 'to take the risk of marching away into the unknown without exactly knowing where we were or how to get back'.

Into November, and they began to be troubled by high winds and the consequent frost-bite. The sledge runners needed constant attention. On 4 November Scott tells of how the weather suddenly turned vicious – 'the full force of the gale burst upon us, and the air became thick with driving snow'. The runners of the sledges had split again and they were hardly able to drag them as they looked desperately for snow soft enough to allow them to pitch camp, 'but everywhere finding nothing but the bare blue ice'. Tented at last, Scott records the temperature as

The Emperor Penguin colony at Cape Crozier, drawn by Edward Wilson on his and Royds' visit there in September 1902.

81

—24 °F, 'and it is blowing a full gale; it is not too pleasant lying under the shelter of our thin, flapping tents under such conditions. ...' Nevertheless, for day after day they had to lie up and suffer. 'It was Wednesday, November 4, when we pitched our tents so hurriedly; it was Wednesday, November 11, before we resumed our march' – what he called 'the most miserable week I have ever spent'.

On 22 November Scott decided to send half the party back under Skelton, going on himself with Lashly and Evans. In the three weeks that followed, Scott wrote,

I do not think it would have been possible to accomplish more. ... Evans was a man of Herculean strength. ... Lashly, in appearance, was the most deceptive man I have ever seen. He was not above the ordinary height, nor did he look more than ordinarily broad, and yet he weighed 13st 8lb, and had one of the largest chest measurements in the ship. ... With these two men behind me, our sledge seemed to become a living thing, and the days of slow progress were numbered.

Temperatures were very low now, —40 °F at night rising some fifteen degrees during the day, and this in the Antarctic summer. The wind, he wrote, 'has cut us to pieces. We all have deep cracks in our nostrils and cheeks, and our lips are broken and raw. . . .' A sense of comradeship grew up between the three men. Scott won the acceptance of his two companions, and the unquestioned social code of the time that strictly separated men from officers gave way before the greater reality of the tremendous wastes, with their silence, their deep crevasses, their sudden stands of scoured rocks, their screaming winds and brilliant, unexpected days of sunshine. The three men shared one sleeping bag at night, their warmth, given and taken, an unspoken pact ensuring their survival. By day they bent together, struggling in the same harness, facing the same problems.

On 30 November Scott called a halt; they had decided to continue westward until the end of the month, and they had done so.

We have finished our last outward march, thank heaven! ... The scene about us is the same as we have seen for many a day, and shall see for many a day to come – a scene so wildly and awfully desolate that it cannot fail to impress one with gloomy thoughts. I am not an imaginative person, but of late all sorts of stupid fancies have come into my mind. ... My companions spare no time for solemn thought. ... Few of our camping hours go by without a laugh from Evans and a song from Lashly.

OPPOSITE Scott about to set off on a depot-laying journey, Mount Erebus in the background. The first of *The Illustrated London News'* photographs.

'Turning into a three-man sleeping bag'; sketch by Edward Wilson.

They made good time as they began their journey back to *Discovery*, although a week later Scott was writing, 'Hunger is growing on us once more.' They were hampered by the surface, here *sastrugi*, the convoluted ridge-backed waves of frozen snow which went on for mile after mile, there the granulated flakes of the new falls which ripped at sledge runners like sand, 'I have done some hard pulling, but never anything to equal this', Scott wrote later. On the 12th he noted that 'we have been pulling ten hours a day; it is rather too much when the strain on the harness is so great, and we are becoming gaunt shadows of our former selves.' They were still fit, however, although troubled by 'pangs of hunger which are now becoming exceedingly acute'.

On 14 December the party passed what they all agreed was 'the most adventurous day in our lives'. Balked by a rough surface, they cast about for an easier route, then stopped to discuss their situation – should they halt, which 'might mean another long spell in a blizzard camp, when starvation would stare us in the face', or should they go on, seeing only with difficulty through the drifting snow the dangers which faced them? It was decided to go on; soon they were threading their way 'amongst the hummocks and across numerous crevasses'.

After a while they found themselves on a smoother slope and the sledge began to run. Lashly and Evans were harnessed behind it to check its speed, the surface became more and more icy, foothold harder and harder to keep. 'Suddenly Lashly slipped, and in an instant he was sliding downwards on his back; directly the strain came on Evans, he too was thrown off his feet ... before I had time to look the sledge and the two men hurtled past me; I braced myself to stop them, but might as well have attempted to hold an express train.' All three hurtled down the slope, the sledge amongst them; as the ground became rougher they began to be bounced and bundled to and fro by its irregularities. Scott records that he thought they were bound to end with broken limbs, 'for I felt we could not stand much of such bumping'. Yet stand it they did, landing after a final terrifying lurch and leap into the air which brought them down with tremendous force on a gradual incline, stopping there at last, held by the very roughness of the snow which had been their greatest danger, struggling bruised but intact to their feet. The accident had an unexpectedly good outcome: 'As soon as I could pull myself together I looked round, and now to my astonishment I saw that ... ahead and on either side of us appeared well remembered landmarks. . . .' His pleasure was somewhat premature; they had survived a tumbling fall of three hundred feet, but the day was not over yet.

They moved on; they had lost most of their provisions but had come within reach of their next depot. Late in the afternoon they were no more than six miles from this haven stuffed with waiting plenty, Scott in the middle, bent over his trace, Lashly to his right, Evans to his left. A gust of wind swung the sledge round, Lashly moved out to steady it; abruptly 'Evans and I stepped on nothing and disappeared from his view; by a

Camp below the peaks
guarding Antarctica's
landmass.

miracle he saved himself from following, and sprang back with his whole weight on the trace. . . . Personally, I remember absolutely nothing until I found myself dangling . . . with blue walls on either side and a very horrid looking gulf below. . . .'

He called to Evans 'and received a reassuring reply in his usual calm, matter-of-fact tones' – a tribute to the Petty Officer's phlegm, since he too was hanging in that chilling nowhere. Scott reached out, swung, found no foothold, swung further, all the time doubtless conscious of how easily the wedged sledge above them might give. At last he found a slab of ice which had become jammed between the otherwise smooth walls, and managed first to transfer his own weight to it and then to manœuvre Evans into place beside him. Lashly, in his usual laconic way, describes what happened then: 'After they were safely dangling down there in space I at once secured the sledge with a pair of ski, and held on to the other end while the Captain climbed up out. Rather a difficult thing to do especially as his hands were getting frost-bitten all the time. We then pulled Evans up and once more proceeded on our way. . . .' Scott, more involved or perhaps better able to set into words what he had experienced, put it more loquaciously;

I must confess I never expected to reach the top. . . . But it was no use thinking about it, so I slung my mitts over my shoulders, grasped the rope, and swung off the bridge. I don't know how long I took to climb or how I did it. . . . Then, mustering all the strength that remained, I reached the sledge itself and flung myself panting on the snow beyond. Lashly said 'Thank God!' and it was perhaps then I realised that his position had been the worst of all.

And he records that when he and Lashly had managed to haul Evans to the surface, that contained individual said only, 'Well, I'm blowed' – 'it was the first sign of astonishment he had shown.'

During the remaining days Lashly had an attack of snow-blindness, but on Christmas Eve they arrived back on board *Discovery*. 'And so', Scott says, 'after all our troubles and trials we spent Christmas Day in the snug security of our home quarters'; in the eighty-one days of their journey the three men 'had covered 1,098 miles, at an average of 15.4 miles a day and, not including minor undulations, we had climbed heights which totalled to 19,800 feet. . . . I devoutly hope that wherever my future wanderings may trend, they will never again lead me to the summit of Victoria Land.'

The other sledging parties had had varying success; Ferrar, the geologist, had managed to gather a large number of rock samples, many of them from almost inaccessible places; Barne and Mulock, travelling south in the footsteps of Scott's party of the previous year, had found themselves held back by incredible head winds, yet had nevertheless managed to map some more of that distant, 'immensely disturbed' coastline which Scott and his companions had been the first to see; Royds had led a party south-east, during which, for night after night, Bernacchi took magnetic observations inside the only tent, while for up to an hour his companions stood patiently about in the Antarctic cold; Wilson had travelled to Cape Crozier to take another look at the penguins, and had then gone with Armitage to chart the topography and movement of the glacier named after the expedition's other doctor, Koettlitz. As Scott put it, 'my companions had been working diligently in every direction which promised to increase our store of information.'

While he had been away Armitage had also begun the labour of trying to free *Discovery* from the surrounding ice. For days teams of men had been hauling at the ropes which worked the eighteen-foot ice saws, but when on 2 January 1904 Scott went to see how they were getting on, 'I found that the result of twelve days' solid work was two parallel cuts 150 yards in length. . . . The ice was between six and seven feet thick, and each stroke only advanced the saw a fraction of an inch. . . . Our sawing efforts have been an experience, but I'm afraid nothing more.' Scott decided that he could do no more than hope that tide and weather would be more lenient with his ship this year than they had the year before.

On 5 January while on a short field trip with Wilson, happy amongst the ice and the penguins – 'I have come to the conclusion that life in the Antarctic can be very pleasant' – Scott was sitting in contemplative mood in the tent, reclining, considering the day, digesting his breakfast. 'Our tent door was open and framed the clear sea beyond, and I was gazing dreamily out upon this patch of blue when suddenly a ship entered my field of view.' The relief ship had come; the two men began hastily to gather up their things. 'Whilst we were thus employed, Wilson looked up and said, "Why, there's another." . . . We had of course taken for granted that the first ship was the *Morning*, but what in the name of fortune could be the meaning of this second one?'

Winter quarters at Hut Point, with the ice-bound *Discovery* in the background.

Equipment being transported
from the *Discovery* across the
ice to the relief ships.

It would in a sense be true to say that the second ship had very little meaning; if it signified anything it was the lack of confidence that was felt in Scott by the men now in charge in London, and the total lack of efficiency with which they had gone about their own hurried operations. In addition to *Morning*, they had bought *Terra Nova*, an old whaler, and had then had her towed by relays of warships through the Mediterranean, the Suez Canal and the Indian Ocean all the way to New Zealand, an inelegant and wasteful means of transportation made necessary by the lack of time they had left themselves.

This cumbersome, double-headed relief expedition, commanded once more by Colbeck, now transmitted to Scott the Admiralty's arbitrary instruction that if *Discovery* were not freed in time she would have to be abandoned. Scott was dumbfounded; as he says, 'the ties of sentiment which bound us to the *Discovery* were very far beyond the ordinary ... the thought of leaving her had never entered our heads'. Open water was twenty miles away, the retreat from the Antarctic was scheduled for six weeks hence – it seemed improbable that the ice would give way in time. On 10 January, back in the trapped *Discovery*, Scott 'assembled all hands on the mess-deck, where I told them exactly how matters stood. There was a stony silence. I have not heard a laugh in the ship since I returned.'

Mail, parcels and necessary supplies passed from the relief ships across the ice to *Discovery*; the expedition's equipment began to make the reverse journey, all in an atmosphere of some melancholy. Near Hut Point the ice saws were still busy, but the solid surface looked no nearer breaking up. *Terra Nova* began to attack the edge of the ice field itself, but on 23 January Scott noted that 'she could make no impression on the solid sheet, though she rammed it full tilt'. On the 28th, however, the whole sheet began to sway with the movement of the long swell under it; over the next few days the ice began to break up on the seaward edge of the field. By 1 February Scott could write, 'We seem to be hanging in the balance, with even chances either way.' Six days later he began to blast a way through, although with little immediate effect. On the 10th he wrote, 'I have made every arrangement for abandoning the ship.' But four days later he was brought running from his dinner by the shout from the deck, 'The ships are coming!' The whole of the ice sheet was breaking apart – 'without an effort on our part it was all melting away, and we knew that in an hour or two not a

FURTHEST SOUTH

THE ADVENTUROUS VOYAGE OF THE "DISCOVERY," AND THE SLEDGE JOURNEY TO THE FURTHEST POINT SOUTH EVER REACHED BY MAN.

BY LIEUTENANT E. H. SHACKLETON, ONE OF THE THREE OFFICERS WHO REACHED THE MOST SOUTHERLY LATITUDE YET ATTAINED.

AS IS WELL KNOWN, the National Antarctic Expedition left England in August 1901 for scientific work in the Southern oceans, having been fitted out under the auspices of the Royal Society and the Royal Geographical Society. The officers and men were lent by the Admiralty from the Navy and Royal Naval Reserve. A grant of £45,000 was made by the Government specially to aid the magnetic work, which was one of the most important parts of the Expedition. Passing over the outward voyage, during which the ordinary incidents of sea-travel occurred, we come to the departure of the *Discovery* from Lyttelton, New Zealand, on December 21. Ten days after leaving, the ship *Discovery* had her first experience of the ice when she entered the *pack*. Pack-ice, or the pack, is the ice that has formed on the sea and in sheltered bays during the winter, and, with the approach of summer, assisted by snow and gale, works up and floats away to the northward in a more or less dense mass, that finally dissolves in the warmer waters of the lower latitudes. Fortunately, the pack at this

THE HEADQUARTERS OF THE MAGNETIC SURVEY, ONE OF THE CHIEF OBJECTS OF THE EXPEDITION: THE MAGNETIC HUT, WITH THE "DISCOVERY" IN WINTER QUARTERS IN THE BACKGROUND.

PHOTOGRAPH BY LIEUTENANT SHACKLETON.

In this hut one of the most important duties of the Expedition, that for which the Government gave £45,000—magnetic research—was carried out. Observations were taken every two hours, in all weathers. At the door of the hut is Mr. Bernacchi, the expert in electrical science.

vestige of it would be left. . . .' And with the break up of the ice, the other two ships were closing the gap between themselves and the expedition base, buffeting aside the creaking floes, charging through, then twisting to and fro as they searched for clear water and tried to open and preserve a channel. By the 15th ropes had grappled *Morning* to *Discovery*; on the 16th the last charges of gun-cotton were fired and 'in another minute there was a creaking aft and our stern rose with a jump as the keel was freed from the ice which had held it down. . . . Thus it was that after she had afforded us shelter and comfort for two full years . . . our good ship was spared to take us homeward.'

OPPOSITE The significant heading of *The Illustrated London News'* feature on Scott's expedition. The photograph shows Bernacchi at the door of the hut designated for magnetic research, a project supported by the government with a sum of £45,000. The ice-bound *Discovery* can just be seen in the background.

3
Arrival

As the news reached London that Scott had at last arrived in New Zealand, it became clear that he had now become to some extent a celebrated man. For the moment dissension was bridged over by praise; *The Times* pointed out to the world on 2 April 1904 that 'this great national expedition is bringing home with it a mass of data and a store of collections that will throw a flood of light on the darkest area of our globe so far as human knowledge is concerned'. And it is true that Scott and his men had travelled further upon the main mass of Antarctica than anyone before, in the process drawing new and more detailed maps, carrying out a widespread topographical survey, charting the variations in the weather, taking endless magnetic readings, examining the extent, structure and movement of the ice shelf and of individual glaciers, adding enormously to the zoologists' knowledge of the area's fauna, particularly of the life cycle of the appealing penguin; and, beyond all that, offering new and inspiriting evidence of human endurance and adaptability in conditions which had for millennia denied man the slightest foothold, the most rudimentary acceptance.

At the same time as Scott, other expeditions had been busy in the Antarctic: the Germans under von Drygalski, the Swedes under Nordenskjöld, the French under Charcot, the Scots under Bruce. Drygalski had spent over a year in the area and discovered Kaiser Wilhelm II Land, as well as taking photographs from the Antarctic's second balloon; the Swedes, despite losing their ship on the way home, did very valuable scientific work north of Graham Land; Charcot made definitive charts of many parts of the Palmer Archipelago; while Bruce penetrated into the bleak and dangerous Weddell Sea, there finding, although not exploring, a coastline he named after his expedition's sponsor: Coats Land. (In a fit of justifiable pique at the British Government's refusal to help support his work, Bruce also turned over to the Argentines a meteorological station he had founded on Laurie Island, thus causing the Foreign Office a diplomatic headache which the territorial claims and counter-claims still resounding today do nothing to ease.) Yet Scott and his party had worked longer and harder than most of the others, had penetrated much farther south, had done more, and more profitable sledging; as *The Times* put it, dismissively mixing the chauvinistic with the patronising, 'It would be invidious to compare what has been accomplished by the expedition commanded by a British naval officer with what the three other

expeditions that have been simultaneously at work have been able to do.'

Commendation was redoubled when in September *Discovery* secured at Spithead. There was, *The Times* now told its readers,

no one deserving higher praise than Commander Scott himself. As a sailor, he has navigated the *Discovery* with the highest skill and courage in the most difficult circumstances; as an explorer, on excursions from the ship, he has displayed brilliant enterprise, patient perseverance and daring without recklessness to an exceptional degree; above all, as leader he has known how to keep those under his charge in health and spirits. . . .

Probably better appreciated than this measured panegyric was the reception the returning expedition had had as, moving slowly into Stokes Bay in soft autumn sunshine, they discovered

"THE PARSENGER".

LEFT Scott at the height of his social success in 1909.

RIGHT Caricature of Shackleton from *The South Polar Times* of 1902.

RIGHT Dr Edward Wilson, the talented artist and beloved friend of Scott who accompanied him on both expeditions and shared his fate.

an armada clustered in euphoric welcome, yachts and rowing boats, tall masts and stumpy bowsprits, with beyond them the echoing, disciplined cheers of the Royal Navy crashing across the calm from half a dozen anchored ships.

For Scott now it was something of a trying time. He was a secret man who had perhaps both discovered, and drawn further into himself during these two long, lonely years. Suddenly he found himself ground and buffeted by all the processes of publicity, dazed by a cascade of honours – gold medals, promotion in the Victorian Order, the Legion d'Honeur – forced to face a score of dinners, dozens of gaping lecture audiences. Preferable to all these was his naval promotion; he had been made Captain on the day of his arrival in Portsmouth, which must not only have stilled any doubts he may have felt that his voyage to the Antarctic would disrupt or delay his career, but which also offered him a rise in pay he was swift to translate into an increased allowance for his mother.

The pace quickened, became countrywide, after he had lectured at the Albert Hall in front of 7000 people, being presented with gold medals both by Sir Clements Markham and the American Ambassador. His friends now came from a wider world; he met men and women in Society, in the arts and the theatre. He had become a celebrity, one who was invited to dinner to prove how close the host or hostess was to the world's important centre. 'I've had enough of notoriety to last me a lifetime. There has been no peace, no quiet – nothing but one mad rush'; thus he wrote in a letter at about this time.

A little over a year after his return, he himself stepped briefly out of the world of action into the world of literature: 'A masterly work', said *The Times Literary Supplement* when his *The Voyage of the 'Discovery'* was published. By Christmas it was sold out. Given this amount of public enthusiasm Markham now asked the government to acquire *Discovery* for the nation; the reply was the Admiralty's bill to the Royal Geographical Society for naval services rendered. Small wonder that Scott, telling his mother of the reception the King had given him during a visit to Balmoral, wrote with emphatic irony, 'All sorts of nice things were said afterwards, much nicer than by the Prime Minister, who said he regarded himself as the *Father of the Expedition*!!!!' His beloved ship, home, base and prime responsibility for over two years, was sold to the Hudson Bay Company for £10,000; today, however, she lies, more happily and much visited, in the Thames, within sight of the House of Commons which always treated her in so niggardly a fashion.

Scott returned to the Navy, joining HMS *Victorious* in August 1906. On duty in the Mediterranean he met Sir Clements Markham again, the old man and he visiting Majorca together. Did Sir Clements put before him the possibility of a second expedition, dangle the vision of that uninviting but still-to-be-achieved South Pole? They must have discussed it, and such a journey was certainly on Markham's mind. Nor did the news at the end of that year that Shackleton intended to mount an Antarctic expedition help to lessen his ambitions. Regarding Shackleton as a subordinate of his own protegé, Markham saw in the Merchant Marine officer's plans something akin to mutiny.

Shackleton, however, had found his own patron in the person of his employer, Beardmore, owner of a great engineering works in Glasgow. With the industrialist guaranteeing a large

Shackleton on the bridge of his ship the *Nimrod*.

proportion of the money, Shackleton was able to announce his own expedition in February 1907. His ambitions were mixed with patriotism in this for there were rumours that both the French and the Belgians were planning expeditions; the South Pole was rapidly becoming the kind of target for chauvinistic adventure which Mount Everest was to be between the two world wars.

Scott, however, was quietly laying foundations of his own. As early as September 1906 his new friend, the writer J. M. Barrie, had greeted with pleasure hints that 'all the old hankerings' were nagging at Scott once more. Thus Shackleton's announcement of his proposed voyage, swiftly picked up by the newspapers, astonished and irritated Scott. He wrote to Wilson, who in his solid, peace-making way (he must often have kept the balance between the two men on their southern journey) pointed out that he did not believe Shackleton was rushing to forestall Scott in the Antarctic – 'I myself have never heard a hint of your going South again.' Shackleton's consternation equalled that of Scott when he found that Mulock, the man who had taken his place when he had been forced to go home, had already volunteered to go to the Antarctic with his old commander; this was the first news of Scott's intentions that Shackleton had received.

A correspondence began between Shackleton and Scott, the latter writing from somewhere in the Atlantic where he was now serving in HMS *Albemarle*. The area of contention narrowed; Scott, after all, did not have colonial rights over the Antarctic continent, nor had he pre-empted the honour of being first to the South Pole. What he did claim, however, was the Hut Point base in McMurdo Sound. He had established it and he felt it should be his to use once he was ready to do so. On the other hand, Shackleton's appeal for his backers had been precisely his familiarity with Hut Point and the area to the south of it. Wilson, brought in as natural arbiter, wrote to Shackleton, 'I think that if you go to McMurdo Sound & even reach the Pole – the gilt will be off the gingerbread because of the insinuation ... that you forestalled Scott who had a prior claim to the use of that base.' On 4 March in a cable to Scott, Shackleton accepted Wilson's advice to be quixotic.

Scott, however, seems for a while to have demanded more than this, proposals which Shackleton rejected with some irritation: 'I realise myself what I have given up in regard to

J. M. Barrie
Author.

J. M. Barrie, the famous Scottish writer, whose close friendship with Scott dated from their first meeting, when they were reported to have walked the streets of London deep in a conversation that lasted almost through the night.

this matter', he wrote to Scott. 'Concerning the 170 Meridian West as a line of demarcation, this matter will have to be discussed. I must tell you quite frankly ... that I do not see my way, at the present moment, to accede to this. . . . I am ready to discuss with you the whole matter but I want you to understand that I do not look upon either Wood Bay or the land to the West of Cape North as being within the province of any particular previous expedition.' It is hard not to see something grudging in Scott's attitude and yet it is very understandable in view of his vested interest in the area.

Sometime in April Shackleton returned to England after a sledge buying trip to Norway, while Scott sailed in from his Atlantic patrol. The two men met and to some extent managed to clear the air. On 17 May Shackleton set down his proposed sledging routes and made a categorical promise: 'I am leaving the McMurdo Sound base to you, and will land either at the place known as Barrier Inlet or at King Edward VII Land whichever is the most suitable. . . . If I find it impracticable to land at King Edward VII Land or at Barrier Inlet or further to the NE, I may possibly steam north and then to westward and try and land to the west of Kaiser Wilhelm II Land. . . . I think this outlines my plan, which I shall rigidly adhere to. . . .'

It says something of the moral climate of the times, of the code of honour, rather like that once common among duellists, with which that climate had imbued a whole class, that these considerations should have caused so much debate, so much anguish – and in the event so many difficulties, practical and psychological, for Shackleton himself. In any case, Scott replied, acknowledging the agreement – 'If as you say you will rigidly adhere to it, I do not think our plans will clash.'

In the meantime Scott had begun to gather a team for his proposed expedition. Lieutenant Evans, navigating officer in the *Morning*, asked if he could join the group and was accepted. Wilson, when approached, asked with quirkish modesty, 'Can you really mean that you would like me to go South again with you? ... Without a doubt, I should like to go with you.' But Scott's main attention remained on his naval career, which in mid-1907 was in danger of suffering a set-back. His ship, *Albemarle*, during a close-formation exercise with the Atlantic Fleet, was in collision with HMS *Commonwealth*. For a while he was worried, for he knew that a court-martial in which he figured would now attract a great deal of unpleasant attention.

OPPOSITE Lieutant Evans, leader of the Last Supporting Party on Scott's dash to the Pole, destined soon to become, as 'Evans of the *Broke*', a famous war hero and an admiral; photographed here on board the *Terra Nova*.

PAULINE CHASE

Pauline Chase, the beautiful actress whose name became temporarily linked with Scott's.

He was relieved when a court of enquiry reprimanded no one – the fault lay at levels in the hierarchy so high that censure must have seemed to the assembled officers a worse outrage than the original mistake.

For Scott, however, something even more momentous was happening. He had at various times had what were at least friendly relations with young women. In 1887 when still a sub-lieutenant he had come to know Kathleen O'Reilly, daughter of a judge into whose home he was welcomed while serving in HMS *Amphion*, based in British Columbia. He had corresponded with her through all the intervening years. After his Antarctic success, he seems to have blossomed out a little – Mabel Beardsley, sister of the artist Aubrey Beardsley, became almost laughably possessive about him. The actress Pauline Chase, famous for her portrayal of Barrie's Peter Pan, was another girl in whom Scott at this time showed a definite interest. It may be that success, apparently without effect on him, had in fact to some extent loosened his control, made him more open to the external world and its attractions. In any case, it was at this time, in this frame of mind, that he first met Kathleen Bruce.

She was an artist, a sculptress; it is notable that in the world

Theatrical production of 1906 with Mabel Beardsley on the extreme left (foreground) and Pauline Chase third from left.

through which he now moved, famous in his own right, artists figured largely. Writers, actors, painters – it was from among these that he now seemed to pick his preferred friends: in more ways than one he was an unusual naval officer, a man with strange, half-acknowledged hungers in his soul. Kathleen Bruce had newly arrived from Paris where she had lived the life of the untrammelled artist, happy but yet a little suspicious of the freedom it afforded. She knew Rodin, she had become a close friend of Isidora Duncan. Both these were people who believed in the artistic and sexual freedoms which, for them, the life of an artist seemed to demand; one does not know Kathleen Bruce's attitudes to these matters, although the conventions of the time permitted innocence and licence to co-exist quite happily in a certain kind of 'Bohemian' milieu.

She for her part – seated at a luncheon party between Barrie and Max Beerbohm – noticed Scott, a man 'not very young . . . not very good looking, but healthy and alert'. Kathleen herself was tall, vital, with blue eyes and a strong nose, a woman whose energy and presence ensured that she was rarely overlooked. Later that year, Scott asked the hostess (perhaps unfortunately the infatuated Mabel Beardsley) to arrange another meeting;

107

OPPOSITE Kathleen Bruce.

this time Kathleen noticed that he was of medium height, 'with broad shoulders, very small waist, and dull hair beginning to thin, but with a rare smile, and with eyes of a quite unusually dark blue, almost purple. I had never seen their like.'

By November Scott was in love. 'All serious thought goes when I see that sweet face', he wrote to her. 'Dear, if you know I'm half frightened of you. I'm very humbled before you. I've so little, so very little, to offer you.' By the end of the year his mother seems to have understood the seriousness of his feelings; on 31 December she wrote to him, 'You have carried the burden of the family since 1894. It is time now for you to think of yourself and your future.'

Kathleen, however, had her doubts. She had always wanted a son; it seemed to her the only reason why one might marry. 'Now that very thing seems as though it would only be an encumbrance *we* could scarcely cope with', she wrote just after the turn of the year, and it is not their emotional but their financial capacity she is questioning. It is true that Scott, with his small naval pay out of which he allowed his mother £200 a year, had been in the fashion of the times expected to marry someone with money. But Kathleen had other doubts – she thought she and Scott were 'horribly different', and she suggested that they 'abandon the idea of getting married and don't let's look at any more houses. There are things about it I'm not sure I can face.'

Scott remained steadfast, although aware of the financial problems. 'I want to marry you very badly, but it is absurd to pretend I can do so without facing great difficulty. . . . My mother is 67, only a strand of life remains. She has had a hard life in many respects. I set myself to make her last years free from anxiety. I can't lightheartedly think of events that may disturb that decision.' He made calculations – 'Rent £65, rates & taxes £27 . . . servants' wages £45 . . . food for 4 persons at 10s. per head per week £104 . . .' – and came to the conclusion, 'It isn't quite cheerful.' As he wrote that, on 8 January, Shackleton in his *Nimrod*, a week out of Lyttleton, New Zealand, and headed south, was being flung to and fro by the last excesses of a hurricane which had already been blowing for two days; however uncomfortably, Scott's main rival was pressing onwards towards the goal they both so desperately wanted.

In February Kathleen was writing to Scott, 'I do find your love for me so precious, so precious'; in March she concluded a

:: IN TOWN AND OUT ::

make matters more trying still they wait until the climatic conditions render it somewhat difficult even to think and then seize the opportunity of asking us to lay bare before a usually indifferent public all the intimacies of our daily lives, to say nothing of the inner workings of our own souls. Of course, I know well there are a great many people who must either rush into print or go mad, and it is they who probably look to the silly season as the most vital moment of the year. But really, looking over the morning papers every day, as one must do if one wants to keep oneself *au fait*, it is appalling to read with what horrible seriousness this class of persons treat their subject, and in any case it is rather trying to have to thrash out all the very serious subjects in daily life by the middle of September.

MISS KATHLEEN BRUCE

Press Picture Agency

Daughter of Canon Lloyd Bruce, who is engaged to marry Captain Scott at Hampton Court in September

The King's Plans.

IT is expected that King Edward will arrive from the Continent on Saturday, September 5, when he will rest from the fatigues of the return journey by spending the week-end quietly at Buckingham Palace previous to leaving on a visit to Lord and Lady Savile at Rufford Abbey on the following Monday morning. From there he will

The Nobel Prizes.

From all accounts the Nobel prizes for literature will this year be awarded to two Belgian poets, Maurice Maeterlinck and Verhaeren, and the justness of the choice it will not be possible to dispute. M. Maeterlinck is, of course, very well known in London, where a few seasons back his beautiful and accomplished wife, Georgette Leblanc, gave a series of recitations of her husband's poems at the Criterion Theatre, while *Pelléas and Mélisande* has often been performed by Mrs. Patrick Campbell, sometimes in conjunction with Madame Sarah Bernhardt. Of his prose writings the translations by Alfred Sutro have been received everywhere in England with great enthusiasm. As for

CAPTAIN R. F. SCOTT

Who was in command of the "Discovery," and whose marriage to Miss Kathleen Bruce in September is announced

M. Verhaeren, his work is for some unaccountable reason very little known on this side of the Channel. Like his compatriot he too is a dreamer who finds his inspirations among the wild and desolate sea country of ancient Flanders. Both men have the same dreamy, ethereal ideal with which it is impossible to quarrel but which might conceivably send one to sleep.

ABOVE Engagement announcement between Scott and Kathleen Bruce which appeared in *The Tatler*, 26 August 1908.

PREVIOUS PAGES Castle Rock below Mount Erebus; watercolour by Wilson.

letter to him with an abrupt, 'I won't marry you, Con, anyhow. Goodbye, dearest. I love you very, very much.' But in April, after sitting in early sunshine at Kew, she wrote, 'It's these lovely spring days that make you love me so much.' He told her in a letter later that month, 'Kathleen, there is no one like you — never a girl who looked life so boldly in the face. I love your splendid independence and the unswerving directness of you.' It is clear that she was exhilarated by his feelings for her, clear that he held those feelings with a strange mixture of firmness and trepidation; probably, as is so often the case, he could not help himself. His fervour seems uncharacteristic and now and then he checks it, injecting into the correspondence a note of common-sense, sometimes of melancholy, even of self-abnegation. She accepts his love, yet her own mood seems to alter, on occasion abruptly. She comes close, then twists away; she seems to hanker for her freedom, then to hanker for him. She receives his emotions, she is glad of them, yet appears sometimes niggardly with her own.

Nevertheless, when in May Scott was given command of HMS *Bulwark* – 'I shall be the most junior captain in separate command of a battleship' – he lost little time in writing to his mother: 'Now, dear, I must tell you I want to marry Kathleen Bruce – but she and I are agreed that under no circumstances must your comfort suffer. Now all I ask of you is to get to know the girl I love and to break up this horrid condition of strain in which we have been living. ... I do so want to make for a happier state of affairs all round.' It is probable that the extra £100 a year his new appointment meant was decisive in bringing him to a decision; yet the letter suggests unease, family strife, disagreements. Later in the month, after a meeting between these two women in his life, Scott wrote again, reassuringly, 'Dearest Mother, of course Kathleen loved you. She came back full of her visit to you ... Dear, you said something to Kathleen about your love not interfering with hers. She was touched and puzzled, puzzled because the thought that she would come between you and I had not entered her head. . . .' Two days later, his mother was writing to him, 'I am quite ready to take your dear one to my heart and to love her as much as I admire her.'

September was chosen as the month they would be married. Kathleen found a house in Buckingham Palace Road and early in July he wrote, 'Hurrah, the house is ours!' Kathleen, wholehearted now, told him, 'Oh, my dear, how lovely we are going to make everything. You and me. You and me. You and me. I've always been just *me* before. Now it's you and me and it's *good*.' But Scott's self-doubts emerged again in a letter he wrote later that month. 'Girl, I'm a little frightened, vaguely. You're so uncommon and I so conventionalised.' She had, he told her, 'glowing independence of thought' – how would that 'sort with the disciplined, precedent-seeking education of a naval officer? ... Will many things be for one and not for the other? ... I pause to wonder if I have a soul that such a freethinking creature as you could ever find companionable. The distrust is all for myself, remember. I never distrust you.' But he knew himself to

The crew of Shackleton's *Nimrod* expedition.

be more of a person than that, less of a uniformed automaton trapped in the moils of discipline and protocol. He had caught glimpses of himself, a man given to introspection who had faced hardship, danger, even death, in the midst of the world's most appalling desolation. In his next letter he pointed out that 'at forty the reserve of a lifetime is not easily broken. It has been built up to protect the most sensitive spots.'

Now it was she who reassured him – 'I don't believe you love me a bit, or you wouldn't have all those qualms about the ridiculous myth of "the future" ' – and his doubts faded or were

114

packed away. On 2 September 1908 they were married, by the King's permission in the Chapel Royal, Hampton Court. A hundred guests came to the reception, the honeymoon was spent in Etretat on the Channel coast of France; but to its wedding report *The Times* added the statement that 'the marriage will make no difference to Capt. Scott's future plans with regard to Antarctic exploration'.

Among these plans was a vision Scott had of using motorised transport during his polar dash. He had watched at Lautaret, near Grenoble, the trials of a motor-propelled sledge. Built in workshops at Finchley on the outskirts of London by an engineer named Hamilton, these sledges used a threaded steel band which ran over the wheels rather like the later caterpillar track. Lord Howard de Walden put up money for the project and later took out patents on it, but the vehicles proved more attractive in conception than in practice. It was while on the way back from these unsatisfactory Alpine trials that Scott, idly reading the continental edition of the *Daily Mail* in Paris, came across the latest, startling news from the Antarctic: Shackleton, unable to make his planned landing, was after all moving westwards to McMurdo Sound.

Scott was furious; there had been, he felt, a breach of faith so grievous that it would justify his making Shackleton's agreement with him public – 'I propose to let certain persons see the letter', he wrote to his mother in March 1908. To Kathleen he was blunter, sending her a copy of the agreement and commenting angrily that Shackleton had 'just gone bang through it, with unanswerable breach of faith. I had a suspicion he might, and find others had the same, also bit by bit I get evidence of similar actions in his history during the past few years. He seems ... to have thrown scruples to the wind.' This slightly unworthy tirade, allowing nothing for the practical pressures which bear upon the leader of an Antarctic expedition – pressures which he knew better than anyone – reveal by implication some of the ambition which, controlled, channelled, concealed, blazed within Scott; he wanted to be the first man at the South Pole. Almost as much, it seems, he wanted that first man not to be Shackleton. His tone of self-righteous fury contrasts with that of Shackleton himself.

Under the dateline, 'Towards Mount Erebus, 26th Jan.', he wrote to his wife,

Ernest Shackleton with his
wife, Emily, whom he
married in 1904.

Child o'mine I have been through a sort of Hell since the 23rd and I cannot even now realise that I am on my way back to McMurdo Sound and that all idea of wintering on the Barrier or at King Edward VII Land is at an end, that I have had to break my word to Scott and go back to the old base, and that all my plans and ideas have now to be changed and changed by the overwhelming forces of Nature.

He describes his desperate efforts to make the landfall his plans had prescribed, and the heavy ice which everywhere foiled him, then tells her that 'if I had not promised Scott that I would not use "his" place, I would then have gone to McMurdo Sound with a light heart but I had promised and I felt each mile that I went to the West was a horror to me. . . .' Balloon Inlet, above which Scott and Shackleton had floated only a few years before, appeared to have vanished and this made it clear to Shackleton that

any idea of wintering on any other part or inlet of the Barrier would be suicidal. . . . My private word of honour my promise given under pressure was the one thing that weighed in the balance. . . . I told England [the Captain of *Nimrod*] that if I could not get East within 48 hours I would turn back for McMurdo Sound as there was no other place I could go . . . for I have only my word to Scott against my promised plans to the whole world and my 40 comrades.

England had already put to him the dangers and problems that faced them, he and Shackleton both very conscious of 'the laughing careless crowd of men who little thought or dreamt what our feelings were as the ice was closing in'. The whole letter is heavy with Shackleton's anguish, his attempt to justify himself, to still his own sense of guilt – 'My conscience is clear but my heart is sore' – its tone very far from what one would expect from a man Scott was categorising as a 'plausible rogue' who had introduced 'a terrible vulgarising' into 'the Southern field of enterprise, hitherto so clean and wholesome'.

This was not Scott's only period of controversy. In 1908, the first volumes of the collated observations of the *Discovery* expedition began to appear. At once an old argument was revived; Charles Chree, President of the Physical Society, asked that any future leader of a party sent to explore Antarctica should be a scientist who would not be 'overshadowed by the doers of exploits which appeal to the popular imagination'. Later that year Napier Shaw, Director of the Meteorological Office, made some scathing, and possibly unfounded, criticisms of the way weather observations had been gathered; he thought the

Shackleton's hut in
Backdoor Bay near Cape
Royds, the base of
Shackleton's Antarctic
expedition of 1907.

Shackleton and his party beside the Union Jack
that marked the conclusion of their record dash
south, 112 miles from the Pole.

methods used had been incompetent, their inaccuracy compounded by the inexperience of those who used them. It is doubtful if he had properly realised the conditions under which Antarctic explorers had to work; Scott, on the other hand, may have been too aware of them. In any case the Secretaries of both the Royal Society and the Royal Geographical Society urged Scott to keep cool, since public controversy could only bring the whole expedition into disrepute. Scott must have been somewhat comforted by paragraphs in *Nature* which praised the zoological results the expedition had brought back; in the same issue, however, Gregory, once to be leader of the *Discovery*'s scientific team, was rather more lukewarm about some of the physical observations.

Scott had his wife to buoy him up now, his love for her continuing strong, deep and in a curious way astonished: 'I'm priviledged beyond all men. You're so exalted, I somehow can't reach up', he wrote to her in November. (In the Antarctic, Shackleton and his support party were struggling southward now, their ponies, each heaving at over 600 lb, sinking up to their bellies in soft snow.) He tried to define his relationship with Kathleen, to pin down the differences between them: 'Isn't this the pith – to you, it's you and I and a friendly world; to me, it's you and I and the rest inimical.' He wrote of her sculpture, 'My dear, dear heart, there's something so astonishing fine about your work, such truth and vigour, that you must go on.... Your art is too good to be spoilt by notions of gain.' (The day before he wrote that, on 7 December, Shackleton, already a long way past Scott's 'furthest south', suffered what was perhaps the decisive set-back to his plans: his last pony, Socks, fell to instant death in a chasm of ice.)

On 4 January 1909, Kathleen wrote to Scott, 'My very, very dear love, I'm getting so excited and frightened.' The cause of these turbulent emotions was her newly-confirmed pregnancy. She imagined herself the mother of a daughter; she intended calling the girl Griselda – 'I have christened her, given her godparents, estimated her wardrobe, designed her tiny trousseau, educated her and soon shall have married her. Oh, dear, oh, dear, it's too wonderful.' (In the Antarctic, Shackleton and his three companions were pushing desperately on to the Pole from their last depot; by the 9th Shackleton was writing in his diary, 'The last day out we have shot our bolt and the tale is 88°23′s, 162°E.' He had fallen short by 112 miles.)

Scott was now recommended for the post of Naval Assistant to the Second Sea Lord. He accepted it, knowing that it would allow him to be near Kathleen during the months of her pregnancy. But the strange melancholy from which he had always suffered attacked him again. He wrote to Kathleen about it. 'I seem to hold in reserve something that makes for success and yet to see no worthy field for it and so there is this consciousness of a truly deep unrest.' In some ways it seems as though he were exploring his own motives for the deeds he was yet to do. When she went to Paris, happy in the thought of her coming baby, happy to be again exploring the arenas of her art student days and to renew her friendship with Isadora Duncan, he told her in a letter that to her he must be 'the representative of convention', a phrase from his old vocabulary of self-doubt.

Scott's Admiralty appointment began on 24 March (three days before Shackleton arrived back in New Zealand to face the cheering crowd come to the Lyttleton dockside to welcome him). It meant office work from ten till five; the rest of his time was now taken up with the gathering work of his own approaching expedition. Wilson had already agreed to join him; now Lashly and Petty Officer Edgar Evans rallied again to their old leader. And behind Scott there still lurked the influential, energetic presence of the ageless Sir Clements Markham.

With some difficulty Scott was persuaded to meet Shackleton when the latter arrived, to enthusiasm and all the fuss and paraphernalia of fame, at Charing Cross station. The two men

Cartoon of a dancing class of Isadora Duncan, the famous dancer, and friend of Scott's wife.

shook hands; unrecognised, Scott walked away through crowds straining to watch Shackleton pass in an open carriage. If it was galling to him to think that the man he had once sent home in some (at least implied) ignominy had now surpassed his own thrust to the Pole by well over four hundred miles, he gave no indication of it.

Others were less restrained. Markham declared roundly of Shackleton's proclaimed 'furthest south', 'I do not believe it'; he did so in a letter to the then President of the Royal Geographical Society rather than in public, since he held the cause of Antarctic exploration too dear to besmirch it by unseemly argument. It was certainly not Markham who put out the unlikely story that Shackleton had falsified his figures, a rumour which, faintly, has persisted until today.

Scott himself wrote formally to Shackleton about his own proposed voyage: 'I am sure you will wish me success; but of course I should be glad to have your assurance that I am not disconcerting any plan of your own.' Shackleton primly acknowledged Scott's letter and agreed that no plan of his would be interfered with.

Later that summer, however, Scott became acutely aware that he had other rivals elsewhere in the world. In Germany, Japan, Belgium, Norway and the United States expeditions were being planned or already in preparation. The South Pole had become a prize in that mounting struggle between competing patriotisms which was such a feature of the early years of this century, and to be the first to reach it would vindicate the claims of one's country to greatness.

On 13 September the British Antarctic Expedition opened an office in Victoria Street. 'The main object of this Expedition', wrote Scott in a full outline of his plans, 'is to reach the South Pole, and to secure for the British Empire the honour of this achievement'. His purely exploring intentions would be to look at King Edward VII Land, to examine more thoroughly the ice shelf and to extend what knowledge there was of the highlands of Victoria Land. Adding that he expected very extensive scientific work to be undertaken, he appealed for funds, estimating the expedition's expenses at £40,000.

The following day, 14 September, Kathleen gave birth to a son. While she was still a student in Paris, she had told a friend, 'A son is the only thing I do quite surely and always want.' Teased about the young men she knew, she replied, 'None is worthy to be the father of my son.' Now, as she was to write later, she 'fell for the first time gloriously, passionately, wildly in love with my husband'.

Scott meanwhile was beginning to settle to a round of furious work and fund-raising. This time he would be leading, not an official expedition sponsored by august organisations, with the government in shadowy support, but one which depended on the value that people placed on his name; it would be a personal venture. In December he went on half-pay, leaving his post at the Admiralty in order to trot about the country, raising money at meetings and lectures. He resolved to buy *Discovery* again, but was balked by her new owners, the Hudson Bay Company. He settled instead for the *Terra Nova*, the relief ship which had so disconcerted him five years before.

He motored up and down the country; he spoke in Redcar, in Harrogate, in Wolverhampton, in Middlesborough, in York. His talks brought in money, sometimes in dribbles, sometimes in a spate. Manchester gave him more than £2000, Bristol £740, Newcastle an even thousand. Lieutenant Evans, now his second-in-command, also surged about the land, picking off the tycoons, the industrialists, the philanthropists and patriots, coming back with their promises and cheques and notes of hand. The government announced a grant of £20,000; nevertheless, the fund was short of its target. Nor was all friendship and euphoria; people asked Scott at his meetings what the point was of travelling to the Pole. Others wondered why money should be spent on such a project when there was poverty and unemployment in Britain. *Vanity Fair* argued that it had no objections to the Government grant, 'but there is no need to associate it with rubbish about human progress and the advance of civilisation'. Writing to his agent in New Zealand, J.J. Kinsey, Scott said, 'Completing the funds of the Expedition is arduous work.' Nevertheless in March he took Kathleen to Norway to watch trials of a new motorised sledge, one which had taken the place of Hamilton's early and unsuccessful vehicle. Made by Wolseley, this sledge put down a genuine track which anchored itself in snow, thus providing real drive; Scott watched it haul 3000 lb up a slope of nearly one-in-five, its 12 hp engine giving few indications of effort.

Nansen again advised Scott on the use of dog teams, which the Norwegian still thought the most sensible means of polar transportation. During the same visit Tryggve Gran, a skiing

Scott testing a motorised sledge at Fefor, Norway.

124

Taylor and Debenham, two of the members of the scientific staff headed by Edward Wilson, with Gran, the skiing expert.

expert, was invited by Scott to join his expedition and on Nansen's advice he accepted. Back in London other men applied, some old friends, some ex-shipmates, some mere hopefuls with a great variety of skill and experience, not all of it relevant: altogether, some 8000 men volunteered. Wilson, made head of the scientific staff, also began to put together his team; two of them, Taylor and Wright, demonstrated their fitness by walking the fifty miles from London to Brighton. Others were chosen over the next few months – notably stocky little 'Birdie' Bowers who started life as a merchant seaman, then joined the Indian Marine, at one time commanding a gunboat on the Irrawaddy River; the naval surgeon Atkinson; and Meares, the restless globe trotter with experience of Himalayan snow who was to take charge of the dogs.

Scott through his work at the Admiralty had become increasingly aware of the tension which was now beginning to grip Europe. Visiting the offices of the *Daily Mail*, he asked the editor what he thought of the likelihood of war. With almost uncanny prescience, the editor predicted a German strike in the summer of 1914. Scott considered this, then nodded. He would, he said, be entitled by then to command a battle cruiser – 'The summer of 1914 will suit me very well.' It gave him four years from the time of his now planned departure in August 1910.

Money was still a problem. Scott was short of his target, and even that sum was beginning to seem inadequate. 'I do not think £40,000 will see us through', he wrote to Kinsey; he was worried over the £8000 he needed to guarantee full salaries for

Bowers, Cherry-Garrard, Oates, Meares and Atkinson in the 'tenement' bunks of their hut, photographed in 1911.

those who came with him. Not all demanded to be paid; the solid, reliable, utterly honourable Captain Oates from the Army and the young Oxford graduate Apsley Cherry-Garrard put in £1000 each and took no money; their title was 'adaptable helpers', and while Oates later became indispensable with the ponies, Cherry-Garrard found himself Wilson's assistant as zoologist. Lieutenant Campbell, first mate of the *Terra Nova*, also did his work for no pay; Lieutenant Bruce, Scott's brother-in-law, accepted a shilling a month as a token salary. The ship herself was re-rigged, largely by volunteer labour, the necessary alterations she underwent being constantly circumscribed by

Captain Scott and some of his men on board the *Terra Nova* as she sailed from England on 1 June 1910.

lack of money. Petty Officers of the Royal Naval Volunteer Reserve worked enthusiastically on her, giving up free hours at the weekends. From time to time they might have glanced across West India Dock to where the *Discovery* lay, being loaded for a North American voyage under the flag of the Hudson Bay Company. Meanwhile Scott had been made a full member of the Royal Yacht Squadron (an honour which cost the expedition fund £100); this allowed him to register *Terra Nova* as a yacht, avoiding bothersome Board of Trade regulations about crew quarters and overloading.

In May Scott addressed a mixed but distinguished audience at the Royal Institution. He considered the arguments over the value of polar exploration: 'People whose knowledge is derived from the sensational Press count success in degrees of latitude. Others have a contempt for all results except those arising from advanced scientific studies in the regions visited. . . . I submit that efforts to reach a spot on the surface of the globe which has hitherto been untrodden by human feet and unseen by human eyes is itself laudable.' The cheers this elicited must have gratified him.

On 1 June the White Ensign (forbidden *Discovery*, but permitted now because of the intervention of Scott's old chief at the Admiralty) was hoisted and the *Terra Nova* moved down-river. As she slowly dipped and swung at the end of her tow-ropes, the merchantmen on either side sent her away with a cacophony of steam-blasted farewells. She called at Cardiff to fill her bunkers with Welsh coal, a gift to the expedition. Here, there was some dissension between Lieutenant Teddy Evans and Petty Officer Edgar Evans, but although the latter got drunk enough after the official banquet to need six men to support his homeward journey, nothing of this broke the smooth surface public esteem demanded. Cardiff produced another £1000 for Scott's fund, then packed Bute Docks on 15 June with clamouring thousands who cheered the dragon-flag of Wales at the mainmast and yelled their bilingual farewells as the three-masted wooden ship, only 187 feet long, turned her iron-sheathed bow towards the Bristol Channel and the open sea beyond.

Ten days later Wilson wrote to Scott from Madeira, first port of call on the way to the Cape, 'You have got a crew of pirates that would be exceedingly difficult to beat – or equal. I have never been with such a persistently cheery lot before.' Less cheerfully, Scott was struggling with the continuing need for money. He was very conscious of the amount still required to guarantee the pay of those who needed it. At the same time, he was aware of how likely was the possibility of failure; he carefully considered what the chances of survival might be if men were to be stranded at McMurdo Sound. On 16 July Scott himself sailed in the mail ship *Saxon* for the Cape. Kathleen travelled with him, having chosen to make the journey despite having to leave her child in someone else's care; she had Mrs Wilson and Mrs Evans for company.

In Cape Town, the party waited for the overdue *Terra Nova*. Expected early in August, she did not arrive until nearly a fortnight later. In her diary, Kathleen noted that Scott 'was very dejected ... He talked over all the possible things that could have happened.' But all that was wrong was what had been known from the beginning – the *Terra Nova* was a slow ship. The delay did little to help Scott with the fund-raising he had hoped to continue in South Africa; the country, despite its gold and diamond millions, raised rather less than had Cardiff – although this did not prevent them from putting up a monument to the explorer in Cape Town as late as 1960.

Scott decided to sail on from Cape Town in the *Terra Nova*. Lieutenant Evans (who had earlier resented Edgar Evans being given charge of skiing equipment) chose to see this as implying a criticism of himself: 'Evans was much upset at Con's decision', Kathleen wrote. It seems a strange pettiness which now and then shows on the surface of a character everyone agreed was impressive, flawing a man destined to become justly famous and of whom Scott wrote, 'I could not have selected a fitter man to be my *alter ego* or to command the ship.' Yet Skelton, engineer with the *Discovery* expedition, had immediately suspected Evans's hand in Scott's rejection of him for the *Terra Nova* voyage; there was this strange jealousy of Petty Officer Evans, now this touchiness over Scott's actions. For a moment, perhaps, the screen of politeness, awe, euphoric memory thins and the human reality shows through; seen in the afterglow of tragedy people tend to become plaster-cast representations of virtue, their flaws obscured by the need not to diminish a noble death. Perhaps it is a tribute to Evans' forcefulness and impact that in him the roughnesses survive such reverential censorship.

In October the *Terra Nova* arrived in Melbourne, and Scott found that not only was Kathleen waiting but, less happily and more fatefully, a cable sent from Funchal, Madeira. It read 'AM GOING SOUTH. AMUNDSEN'. The Norwegian, having been beaten to the North Pole by Peary, had abruptly changed the direction of his projected expedition. Yet it is unlikely that such a switch could have been made overnight; some of the indignation felt by Scott's supporters seems to have been justified. Among those publicly expressing surprise was the now knighted Shackleton; he predicted that Amundsen would not reach the Pole – although he had dogs, 'they are not very reliable'. They had not been for the British; handled by Scandinavians, they seemed animals of quite a different character.

Again the *Terra Nova* sailed on, now making for New Zealand, while Scott remained to try and wheedle money out of circles both governmental and private. He had considerably more success here than he had had in South Africa, partly because a Japanese expedition was preparing to explore King Edward VII Land and Australians felt a certain uneasiness at the prospects this opened. On 22 October, preparing to sail on to New Zealand, Scott wrote to his mother, 'We are doing splendidly – everything goes like clockwork, including our begging. Kathleen is really wonderful.' But to the Melbourne papers he had said a few days earlier, 'We may get through, we may not. We may lose our lives. We may be wiped out. It is all a matter of providence and luck.'

In Lyttleton, where Scott arrived in the *Terra Nova* at the end of October, Amundsen and money were the elements of a common anxiety: years later, Lieutenant Evans (by then an admiral) remarked that they hardly had enough left to pay for all the coal they needed. Yet they managed to fuel the ship and to settle in the remaining stores. On 26 November the Bishop of Christchurch held a noon-day service on *Terra Nova*'s deck, Scott in the gold lace of a naval captain, the last time he was to wear ceremonial uniform. The ship then sailed to Dunedin, where on 28 November Scott joined her (his own tensions not eased by the 'vague and wild grievances', as he called them in his diary, of Lieutenant Evans and the latter's tearful, over-anxious wife).

Kathleen handed Evans four letters which he was to give to Scott on various personal anniversaries and on Christmas Day. On 29 November the *Terra Nova* at last moved off on the last stage of her journey south. A tug came alongside, hung there for a while, then swung away, turned back to Dunedin. On

board were Mrs Evans, Mrs Wilson and Kathleen. In her diary Kathleen later wrote, 'I decided not to say good-bye to my man, because I didn't want anyone to see him look sad.' To Scott's mother, a few days later, she gave the news: 'At last they are off. All in the best of spirits and exceedingly glad to see the last of ports and stopping places. . . . We had some lovely last days together. Climbing over the hills, we got into great training and very fit and merry. I haven't begun to realise that he's really gone yet, and I don't want to. . . .'

Back in June in London on the other side of the world, the *Evening Standard*, writing about the *Terra Nova*'s departure, had set out what must have been her deepest fear: 'We may never see them again.'

4 Apotheosis

ALL THAT FIRST DAY AT SEA the wind blew, increasing steadily in force. By the second day the *Terra Nova* found herself in a force ten gale. She was heavily overloaded, with a deck cargo of thirty tons of coal, two-and-a-half tons of petrol, three enormous crates holding the motor sledges, the ponies and their forage and the thirty-four dogs. Overshadowed by enormous and still growing waves, the wind shrieking about them, the animals snorting, whinnying and howling their dismay, it seemed for a while as though the expedition would not survive even to reach the ice.

The animals suffered terribly. As Lieutenant Evans later wrote, the ship's rolling 'was so terrific that the poor dogs were almost hanging by their chains'. And Scott tells us, 'Tales of ponies down came frequently from forward, where Oates and Atkinson laboured through the entire night' – Oates, whom Evans remembers, 'his strong, brown face illuminated by a hanging lamp as he stood amongst those suffering little beasts . . . on occasions he seemed to be actually lifting the poor little ponies to their feet as the ship lurched. . . .' Nevertheless one pony died that night, another the next day. A dog died, still hanging in its harness; another, washed overboard, was washed back again by the next wave and survived.

At four o'clock in the morning of 3 December, Scott learned that the pumps were becoming blocked. Eventually, in order to clear the coal dust and coagulated oil which had been choking the suctions, Evans climbed down through a hole in the engine-room bulkhead, and did the work by hand – 'Sitting on the keel the water came up to my neck and, except for my head, I was under water till after midnight . . . it was obvious by 4 o'clock in the morning that the pump was gaining.'

Now Scott could write that 'all is well again, and we are steaming and sailing steadily south within two points of our course'. But there had been loss and damage – two ponies, one dog, ten tons of coal, sixty-five gallons of petrol. On the other hand, he had been able to assess the morale and efficiency of the men with him. He must have been more than happy to see how they had faced emergency; 'hope dawns', he had written on the 2nd, 'as indeed it should for me, when I find myself so wonderfully served. Officers and men are singing chanties over their arduous work. . . . Not a single one has lost his good spirits.'

On 9 December the *Terra Nova* found herself among the irregular floes of the ice pack. Scott wrote, 'I had hoped that we

PREVIOUS PAGES The camp at One Ton Depot: photo taken by Scott

OPPOSITE Crowded conditions aboard the *Terra Nova*, the confusion completed by the Siberian dogs chained around the deck.

should not meet it until we reached latitude 66 or at least $66\frac{1}{2}$.'
First storm, now ice well to the north of where it had been
expected; with his penchant for melancholy, Scott may well
have imagined that fortune was already against him. In a letter
to Kathleen, her brother, Wilfrid Bruce, wrote that Scott was
worried about this pack ice – 'He talked very little to anybody',
while Cherry-Garrard records, 'Delay was always irksome to
Scott. As time went on this waiting in the pack became almost
intolerable.' Not only that, but Scott was also faced with a
dwindling supply of coal which their slow, to-and-fro progress
through the leads of open water forced them to consume at an
unexpectedly high rate. Every time they were stopped, he had
to make a choice of raising steam, banking the fires or letting
them go out. No wonder that by 21 December Scott was writing,

ABOVE Captain Oates with
his beloved ponies: he spent
many hours in the stables
trying to alleviate the
sufferings of the animals
as the ship was tossed
in heavy seas.

OPPOSITE Meares, in charge
of the dogs, and Oates, who
could frequently be found
beside the blubber stove
cooking bran mashes
for his ponies.

'Oh! but it's mighty trying to be delayed and delayed like this, and coal going all the time. . . .'

Nevertheless the ship's company was not idle. Where the ice was level, Scott had them out at every opportunity, practising skiing under the supervision of the young Norwegian, Gran. Some of the dogs had their first run on ice; soundings were taken, plankton brought aboard for the biologists to study, penguins observed. Scott even turned the ice itself into an object of study, asking that a map should be made of the pack which 'ought to give some idea of the origin of the various forms of floes, and their general drift'.

None of this, however, lifted from Scott the burden of his misery at their situation. On 22 December he wrote, 'No, it looks as though we'd struck a streak of real bad luck; that fortune has determined to put every difficulty in our path.' Four days later he felt, 'It is difficult to keep hope alive. . . . There could scarcely be a more dreary prospect for the eye to rest upon.' Only the quality of the men with him seemed to sustain him: 'I have not heard a harsh word or seen a black look.' And at Christmas he could write, 'A merry evening has just concluded. We had an excellent dinner: tomato soup, penguin breast stewed as an entrée, roast beef, plum pudding and mince pies, asparagus, champagne, port and liqueurs – a festive menu.' Given the fare and the five hours the meal took, it seems a little innocent of him to add, 'It is rather a surprising circumstance that such an unmusical party should be so keen on singing.'

By 27 December Scott could remark, 'Everyone says the ice is breaking up', and by the next day he was adding, 'A visit to the crow's nest shows great improvement in the conditions.' On 29 December he notes, 'At last the change for which I have been so eagerly looking has arrived', and on the following day, 'We are out of the pack at length and at last.' But by the evening, with the *Terra Nova* creeping into the teeth of a blizzard, despondency was settling on him again: 'I begin to wonder if fortune will ever turn her wheel.'

The next day, New Year's Eve, the wind began to drop. At 10 pm the clouds lifted and to the west Scott and his companions could see the peaks of what are now called the Transantarctic Mountains, some of them over a hundred miles distant. On 2 January he sighted an old friend, Mount Erebus, which he estimated as 115 miles away. After an abortive attempt to land at Cape Crozier, where Wilson for one would

On the main-top viewing the entry of
the *Terra Nova* into the ice pack, formed of
floating ice broken loose from the fringe of
the Antarctic continent and drifting north
with the coming of summer.

Unloading of the ill-fated
motor sledge, January 1911.

much have preferred to be based and of which Scott too seems
to have thought well – 'No good!! Alas! Cape Crozier with all
its attractions is denied us' – the expedition pushed on towards
McMurdo Sound.

It had been decided that this time a real base would be built
on land; as with Shackleton's *Nimrod* expedition, the ship would
leave the party to winter, returning with new supplies the
following season. The place Scott decided on was what the
Discovery men had called The Skuary, and which he now
renamed more formally Cape Evans. Here, for six days after
their arrival, they laboured over the construction of what
would be the vital part of their world through the months to
come. The *Terra Nova* was about two miles from the shore and
all the necessary supplies had to be sledged over the intervening
ice. The men got up at five in the morning, fell into their bunks
at midnight. Despite the effort involved, everything went fairly
smoothly, although Scott expressed some disappointment with
the motor sledges, which were 'working well, but not very
well', and on 7 January listed the 'host of minor ills' which now
beset the men – snow-blindness, sore faces and lips, blistered

142

feet, cuts and abrasions: 'there are few without some trouble-some ailment.' The third motor sledge fell through the ice and sank – 'A day of disaster', he wrote. On the other hand, most of the ponies and the dog teams were proving satisfactory, and the loads continued to be rushed from the ship – herself working closer to the shore – to where the wooden bones of the hut were rising into place.

Scott paid a visit to the old *Discovery* hut but was depressed to find it 'in such desolate condition'. He blamed Shackleton and his men for leaving it in such a state – 'It seems a fundamental expression of civilised human sentiment that men who come to such a place as this should leave what comfort they can to welcome those who follow, and finding that such a simple duty had been neglected by our immediate predecessors oppressed me horribly.' His oppression did not last long, for two days later, on 17 January, he and his wintering party were moving into their new hut, 'simply overwhelmed with its comfort'. He wrote in his diary, the italics marking his astonished pride, 'It will be a *fortnight to-morrow* since we arrived in McMurdo Sound, and here we are absolutely settled down and ready to start

Scott leading one of the ponies on to land after their harrowing sea journey. A day later the ponies and dogs were hauling sledges from the ship to the newly built hut.

143

Stacking up supplies at
Scott's camp at Cape Evans,
Mount Erebus in the
background.

on our depot journeys directly the ponies have had a proper chance to recover. . . .' It is no wonder that Cherry-Garrard noted in his diary, 'Scott is very cheery about things.'

During the night of 20 December the *Terra Nova* went aground. With ice breaking up and the wind rising, she had stood out to sea. An iceberg floated and settled into the place she had occupied. Returning, she had searched for new anchorage and in the process gone more or less gently ashore. Less cheery now, Scott wrote, 'My heart sank when I looked at her. . . . Visions of the ship failing to return to New Zealand and of sixty people waiting here arose in my mind with sickening pertinacity. . . .' Despite these forebodings Cherry-Garrard could remark, 'At such times of real disaster he was a very philosophical man' – clearly, he did not allow all he felt to become too easily apparent and in this case it was as well, for the crisis passed. Cargo was shifted, men ran from side to side, the ship began to roll; for a while she hung, still locked, then with engines hard astern, she came off the shallows undamaged.

On 24 January the first part of the depot-laying journey began, hazardous from the start since the early section of the route lay over sea ice, at this time of the year a transitory surface as the ice field is liable to break up and float away. The day after they had used it, their pathway had vanished – had it done so thirty-six hours earlier, it might have delayed the expedition by the length of a whole season. On 26 January, having begun to establish a depot beyond the Barrier edge, Scott and those based at Cape Evans said farewell to the *Terra Nova*. She was off to take a party under Lieutenant Campbell eastward to King Edward VII Land, where they were to explore the peaks and cliffs of that forbidding coast; returning, she would leave reports for Scott's party at Hut Point, then sail northward to New Zealand, bearing news of the expedition, letters, dispatches and those disappointed men whom Scott had, often very reluctantly, decided to send back. Scott, addressing the crew on the afterdeck, 'thanked them for their splendid work. They have behaved like bricks and a finer lot of fellows never sailed in a ship.'

By 30 January Safety Depot, the main cache of stores two miles inland from the Barrier cliffs, had been established and Scott was ready to lead his group of assorted men, dogs and ponies southward. Almost at once they found trouble: 'The ponies sank very deep and only brought on their loads with

146

difficulty, getting pretty hot.' Atkinson, the doctor, developed
sores on his foot which became progressively worse until on 2
February he had to be sent back with Petty Officer Crean –
'very hard on the latter', Scott noted, with the compassion he
always felt for men barred from those deeds of action by which
he himself set so much store. The rest of the party decided that
they should in future move at night when temperatures were
lower, thus finding the surface firmer and making life less
arduous for the ponies.

It was at this time that Scott jotted down one of those lists
he headed 'Impressions', inadvertently producing a sort of
loose blank-verse poem celebrating the Antarctic and the life it
forced its explorers to lead. It includes:

The whine of a dog and the neigh of our steeds.
The driving cloud of powdered snow.
The crunch of footsteps which break the surface crust.
The wind-blown furrows.
The blue arch beneath the smoky cloud. . . .
The gentle flutter of our canvas shelter.
Its deep booming sound under the full force of a blizzard.
The drift snow like finest flour penetrating every hole and corner –
    flickering up beneath one's head covering, pricking sharply as a
    sand blast. . . .
The eternal silence of the great white desert. Cloudy columns of snow
    drift advancing from the south, pale yellow wraiths, heralding the
    coming storm, blotting out one by one the sharp-cut lines of the
    land.
The blizzard, Nature's protest – the crevasse, Nature's pitfall – that
    grim trap for the unwary – no hunter could conceal his snare so
    perfectly. . . .

Not great writing, the images largely obvious, almost banal;
yet he felt it necessary to set them down, bending over his note-
books after the hours of discomfort and drudgery (his first line,
'The seductive folds of the sleeping bag'). There was some vision
of himself involved, some idea he must have had of himself as
more than a naval officer, an expedition leader.

Yet the next entry begins with instant practicality, 'Roused
the camp at 10 pm and we started marching at 12.30. At first
surface bad, but gradually improving.' Before long, however,
he is once more caught up in his easy compassion for the
animals – 'It is pathetic to see the ponies floundering in the soft
patches' – and in the almost metaphysical reaction he has to
the difficulties he faced – 'What extraordinary uncertainties this

147

Day, Nelson and Lashly gathered round the
stove in Shackleton's hut, February 1911.

148

work exhibits! Every day some new fact comes to light – some new obstacle which threatens the gravest obstruction. I suppose this is the reason which makes the game so well worth playing.' What sustained him always was his appreciation of the qualities of those who travelled through these wastes beside him. In a letter to Kinsey written about this time, he says, 'The fellows I have with me are splendid. Wilson is wonderful, and is my right hand throughout, but it would be impossible to better any of them. . . .'

On 5 February Scott was writing, 'The blizzard descended on us at about 4 pm yesterday'; Cherry-Garrard, taking it as a type for such storms, described it later, 'But outside there is raging chaos. . . . Fight your way a few steps away from the tent, and it will be gone. Lose your sense of direction and there is nothing to guide you back.' It was three days before they could continue southward, the ponies beginning to flag and sometimes fall as they progressed. On 13 February two men under Evans turned north, to try and lead the most affected ponies back to safety. Scott and the rest pushed on, trying to get as far as latitude 80°s, where he had determined to set up what came to be known as One Ton Depot. On 17 February, however, he was writing, 'We started to build the depot.' The entry is headed, 'Camp 15. Lat. 79°28½′s.' He had fallen short of his target by something over twenty miles. As the black marker flag begins to flutter on its tall bamboo pole, we with our hindsight feel a frisson, a sort of terror, knowing what those twenty miles were to mean. But Scott was optimistic: 'We shall have a good leg up for next year', he wrote.

Now turning north, they began to make their way to Hut Point, where they would receive news of the *Terra Nova* and the Eastern Party under Campbell. Scott and Meares, Wilson and Cherry-Garrard hurried on ahead with the dog teams, while Bowers, Oates and Gran followed more slowly with the still ailing ponies. By the second day Scott had come across the tracks left by Evans and his earlier, returning party. Two days later crossing an ice field corrugated with pressure ridges, his dog team was, with shocking abruptness, engulfed by a crevasse. 'Ten of his thirteen dogs disappeared as I watched', Wilson wrote in his diary, 'they looked exactly like rats running down a hole; only I saw no hole; they simply went into the white surface and disappeared.' The sledge precariously bridged this abyss, and it was fortunate that one of the three dogs still on the surface was Osman, the team leader, who now braced himself to take the weight of the fallen animals, to which he was still attached. Looking down the men saw, still in Wilson's words, 'a great blue chasm in which hung the team of dogs in a festoon', a picture to which Scott adds the fact that they were, not surprisingly, 'howling dismally'. Two, dropped from their harnesses, had fallen to a lower ledge where, with the stoicism of huskies, they lay curled up, going to sleep. In the meantime, Scott tells us, 'Osman the leader exerted all his great strength and kept a foothold – it was wonderful to see him.'

Luckily Scott had made sure than an Alpine rope was with them. They unshipped it, but for the moment could not think how best to use it. 'Choking sounds from Osman made it clear that the pressure on him must soon be relieved' – which they did by securing the hanging dogs to tent poles stretched across the chasm. Meares went down a little way and fixed the rope to the leading end of the trace. They then began to haul the dogs up, two by two, but it took well over an hour before the eleven dogs still in the traces had been hauled to the surface. That still left the two waiting on the ledge. Scott decided to have himself lowered to them; Cherry-Garrard tells us that 'Wilson thought it was a mad idea and very dangerous. . . . We lowered Scott, who stood on the ledge while we hauled up the two dogs in turn. They were glad to see him, and little wonder!' Less gratefully, the dogs on the surface began to fight amongst themselves – 'I heard dim shouts and howls above', Scott reports – and he had to wait until they had been separated and calmed before he was rescued from the chasm. Cherry-Garrard tells us that Scott was intrigued in a scientific way by the direction of the crevasse, which according to theory should have been at right-angles to their path and not running parallel, as it was. While he was being hauled up 'he kept muttering: "I wonder why this is running the way it is – you expect to find them at right-angles" and when down the crevasse he wanted to go off exploring', a course from which the others dissuaded him, since they 'could see the nothingness below through the blue holes in the shelf'.

On 22 February Scott and his companions reached Safety Camp, where they found 'E. Evans and his party in excellent health, but, alas! with only *one* pony'. Later that day Scott and several of the others travelled to Hut Point for news of the *Terra Nova*, only to find that while they had been on the way,

Atkinson and Crean had picked up the mail bag and carried it off to Safety Camp. Scott therefore turned back again, at that instant perhaps still optimistic, happy with the journey he had just made, happy in the knowledge that the most important of the depots which would lie in a long skein southward had now been set up. His only and unnecessary anxiety was for the safety of Atkinson, who had made the journey to Safety Camp across uncertain sea ice. 'But every incident of the day', he wrote of the moment which now awaited him, 'pales before the startling contents of the mail bag which Atkinson gave me – a letter from Campbell setting out his doings and the finding of *Amundsen* established in the Bay of Whales.'

This bay was the long inlet above which Scott had hung from

Keohane with James Pigg, the one survivor of the three ponies that made the depot-laying journey under Lieutenant Evans, and which became the pet of the expedition. It later made the 500-mile journey south.

Amundsen and the crew of the *Fram*.

his balloon in 1902, and it had been picked as a landing place for Campbell and his Eastern Party. But they had been forestalled; as Wilfred Bruce, in the *Terra Nova*, wrote to Kathleen Scott, his sister, 'We turned the corner into the Bay just after midnight on 4 February. I had just got on the bridge and you can imagine our excitement when we found a ship there, which in two minutes we recognised as the *Fram*! Curses loud and deep were heard everywhere. . . .' After some conversation with the Norwegians, Bruce was recording that 'they all seemed charming men, even the perfidious Amundsen. They had 120 dogs and are going for the Pole! No science, no nothing, just the Pole!' In this he was not being entirely fair to Amundsen, for the secondary journeys organised under his command, especially those undertaken by K. Prestrud, made a number of valuable geographical discoveries; but in the main it was true that the whole expedition had been geared to that single ambition.

There were visits to and fro, Campbell and Pennel going to the *Fram*, Amundsen and his lieutenants to the *Terra Nova*. Scott's geologist, Priestley, one of Campbell's party, records the impression the Norwegians made on him – 'a set of men of distinctive personality, hard, and evidently inured to hardship, good goers and pleasant and good-humoured. All these qualities combine to make them very dangerous rivals, but even did one want not to, one cannot help liking them individually in spite of the rivalry.' He thought their winter quarters in the bay dangerous, but if they in fact proved secure, 'they have unlimited dogs, the energy of a nation as northerly as ourselves, and experience with snow-travelling that could be beaten by no collection of men in the world. . . . I think that two parties are very likely to reach the Pole next year, but God only knows which will get there first.'

Cherry-Garrard says that Scott's diary entry 'quite fails to convey how he felt, and how we all felt more or less' as they read the news of Amundsen's arrival. 'For an hour or so we were furiously angry, and were possessed with an insane sense that we must go straight to the Bay of Whales and have it out

Members of the Scott expedition in the wardroom of the *Terra Nova*.

with Amundsen and his men in some undefined fashion or other there and then.' But the mood passed. Scott writes later that day, 'The proper as well as the wiser course for us is to proceed exactly as though this had not happened.' But he realised that Amundsen represented 'a very serious menace', since he would start sixty miles nearer the Pole, and would be able to do so 'early in the season – an impossible condition with ponies'. One wonders whether Scott was not now regretting his disregard for Nansen's advice and the British lack of real expertise with dogs.

Scott meanwhile was beset by more immediate worries – how to get back to winter quarters at Cape Evans. The ice off Cape Armitage was 'so thin that I doubt if the ponies could be safely walked round'. A four-day march brought him to Corner Camp where he met Bowers and Oates, who had been leading the ponies back slowly from One Ton Depot. Almost as soon as they had started, one pony began to fail; next day it died. 'It is clear that these blizzards are terrible for the poor animals. . . . It makes a late start *necessary for next year*.' Whatever vague forebodings Scott may have had then were augmented by 2 March when he wrote, 'The events of the past 48 hours bid fair to wreck the expedition. . . .'

Scott, seeing the poor condition of the ponies, had decided that they should be taken to the shelter of the *Discovery* building on Hut Point. The dog teams led the way, Bowers, Crean and Cherry-Garrard, with four ponies each harnessed to a sledge, followed in their tracks. In making for Cape Armitage, stopping frequently because of the poor condition of the animals, Bowers became more and more alarmed at the weak state of the ice. Describing later what had happened, he wrote that 'at last came a moving crack, and that decided me to turn back'. He and his companions made camp on what he thought was firmer ice (in the darkness picking curry-powder to make cocoa, a mixture Crean at least drank without concern). He was awakened by a noise at about 4.30 am.

'I cannot describe either the scene or my feelings. . . . We were in the middle of a floating pack of broken-up ice.' One pony had disappeared, their camp was on a floe only thirty yards wide and it was with great difficulty that the three men managed to rescue the two sledges, which rested on a neighbouring floe. He remarked that 'we had been in a few tight places, but this was about the limit'. With the three ponies and all their equipment, they began scrambling from floe to floe in an effort to reach the solid footing of the Barrier itself. 'A 12-foot sledge makes an excellent bridge', Bowers noted. But what he called 'further unpleasantness' now reared a singularly ugly head. Reaching the edge of the ice field, they saw that between themselves and safety there lay some thirty to forty feet of open water. Its dark waves were being thrashed to foam by the great 'killer whales', predators which hunt the seals and penguins of the Antarctic coast and which grow to be some thirty feet in length, with vicious tails at one end and vast, many-toothed jaws at the other. Bowers could see hundreds of these creatures, attracted to the spot by their predicament and 'cruising there with fiendish activity'. Selecting a floe which seemed safer than the others, the three men made the animals and the sledges as secure as they could. Then Crean, having volunteered, set off with a message for Scott while the other two waited. They watched as Crean leaped and scrambled across the heaving ice, finally to reach the Barrier and clamber up its intimidating cliffs.

The day passed slowly, while the whales seemed to approach more and more closely, rising from the water to observe the stranded party, their 'huge black and yellow heads, with sickening pig eyes only a few yards from us'. It was 7 pm when Scott at last appeared, calling down to them, 'My dear chaps, you can't think how glad I am to see you safe!' By this time the floe they were on had come to rest against the face of the Barrier itself, but the steepness of the cliff there prevented them from scrambling to safety. At first Bowers stubbornly refused to leave the animals, but Scott finally ordered the men off and with the aid of a rope they were hauled up the ice face. Using the sledges as makeshift ladders, the equipment was then man-handled up the Barrier, but before the problem posed by the ponies could be solved the ice was again on the move. Attempts were made to tie the floe in place but soon, Bowers noted, 'Our three unfortunate beasts were some way out, sailing parallel to the Barrier.'

It was the next morning before another attempt could be made to rescue them. For a while they could not even be found until, as Scott narrates, 'Bowers, who had taken the binoculars, announced that he could see the ponies about a mile to NW.' Some confusion now ensued, for while Scott was searching for a practicable route up the cliff, the others began to hurry the animals across the floes. One fell in and had to be destroyed.

OPPOSITE TOP Lantern lecture given by Herbert G. Ponting, the photographer of the expedition.

OPPOSITE BELOW Meares relaxing at the pianola.

Later, the same fate overtook a second. In the end only one pony was left to scramble up the improvised path Scott and Cherry-Garrard had dug. This was Nobby, lone survivor of the five which had left One Ton Depot with Bowers. Despondently, Scott writes, 'So here we are ready to start our sad journey to Hut Point. Everything out of joint with the loss of the ponies, but mercifully with all the party alive and well.'

At Hut Point they established themselves despite some discomfort in the building which still stood there. Scott naturally wanted to get back to the main base, but as Bowers put it, 'Cape Evans, though dimly in sight, was as far off as New Zealand till the sea froze over.' On 14 March Griffith Taylor brought to Hut Point another group which had been out on a geological survey; now, in a space thirty-six feet square, sixteen men had to exist, while outside, in the lean-to verandah, the dogs and the two remaining ponies found shelter. Scott fretted as the days of incarceration passed: 'I am impatient of our wait here. ... It is ill to sit still and contemplate the ruin which has assailed our transport. ... The Pole is a very long way off, alas!' His entries tell of his anxious watching over the fickle sea ice: 'The young ice is going to and fro, but the sea refuses to freeze over'; 'It is disappointing to find the ice so reluctant to hold'; then, on 27 March, 'Ice holding south from about Hut Point' and the next day, 'Slowly but surely the sea is freezing over.' Their crowded time, with seven sleeping on the floor, others in the store room and the lean-to, was coming to an end; their monotonous diet – seal liver, fried and eaten with bread and butter, cocoa to drink – could be changed by one burst of activity. In the second week of April that burst came: men and sledges were lowered down the ice cliffs to the now solid ice at sea-level – a bold move, since once down there was little chance that they would get back again. On 13 April they arrived at Cape Evans, filthy, bearded and almost unrecognisable – indeed Ponting, the photographer, thought they were visiting Norwegians.

Ten days later the sun rose for the last time before its long winter plunge. Now everyone settled to their own activities, the various scientists in particular working over their specimens and perfecting their equipment. Specialists were required to give lectures on their subject. The men had a gramophone and a shelf of records, they had books and games; on the whole they seem not to have quarrelled. Cherry-Garrard, discussing the whole three years of the expedition, says, 'To be absolutely

156

Scott working in his tiny cubicle, photographs of
his wife and their baby son lining the walls.

158

accurate I must admit to having seen a man in a very "prickly" state on one occasion. That was all ... undoubtedly a very powerful reason was that we had no idle hours: there was no time to quarrel.' Such a state of affairs, however, did require some self-discipline, and he admits that tiny details did sometimes irritate the men and that diplomacy was on occasion necessary to avoid trouble – he records, for example, when out sledging 'how the loss of a biscuit crumb left a sense of injury which lasted for weeks; how the greatest friends were so much on one another's nerves that they did not speak for days for fear of quarrelling. . . .'

Scott, busy at the collapsible table in his tiny cubicle, six feet square and festooned with the furry or the calibrated paraphernalia of the polar explorer, worked over the details of his projected journey south. On 8 May he offered these plans to his companions, giving their outline in a lecture. He asked for suggestions and modifications; he valued those with him too highly to oppress them with anything as intractable as a decree. At the same time, he watched his companions with a keen and analytical eye, noting down their characteristics as they struck him, trying to sift the material available to him for his drive to the Pole.

On Midwinter Day a new issue of the *South Polar Times* appeared – the third, edited by Cherry-Garrard almost a decade after Shackleton had put together the first. In the evening there was a celebration in the flag-decorated hut, with cake and champagne and speeches. Five days later, Wilson led Bowers and Cherry-Garrard out towards Cape Crozier on the first extensive winter journey that had ever been attempted in Antarctica – their object, to collect the eggs of the Emperor penguin at a particular stage of incubation, these birds having become Wilson's special and perhaps favourite study. The trip lasted five weeks; Cherry-Garrard described it as 'the weirdest birds'-nesting expedition that ever was or ever will be; no words can express its horror'. Temperatures went down to $-70\,^{\circ}$F, once to $-77\,^{\circ}$F. Blizzards raged, at one time tearing away the roof of their storm shelter and leaving them in their sleeping bags to the driving snow. It was so cold that they would ice up in a moment – 'I raised my head and found I could not move it back. My clothing had frozen hard as I stood – perhaps fifteen seconds'; thus Cherry-Garrard described it, late in June. No wonder that Scott, reporting their return on 2 August, said,

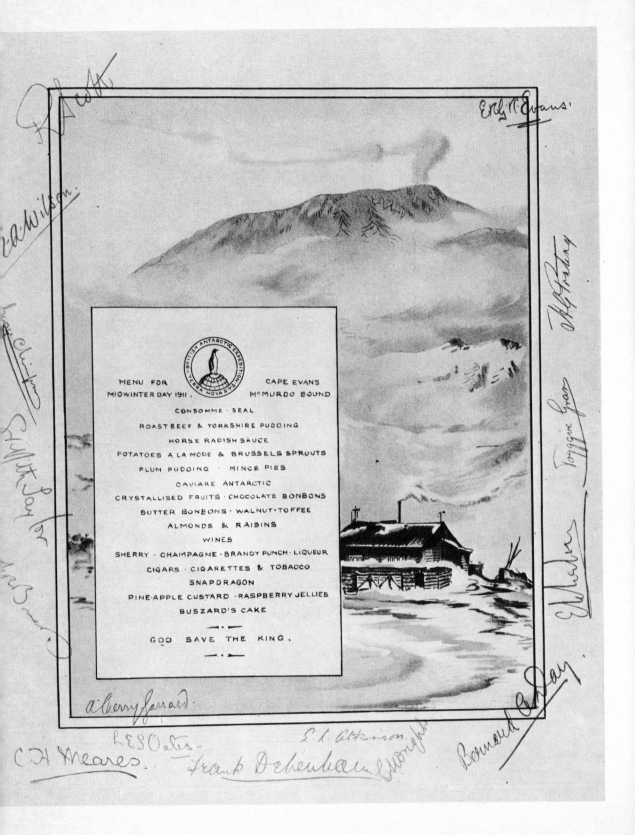

MENU FOR   CAPE EVANS
MIDWINTER DAY 1911.   McMURDO SOUND

CONSOMME · SEAL

ROAST BEEF & YORKSHIRE PUDDING

HORSE RADISH SAUCE

POTATOES A LA MODE & BRUSSELS SPROUTS

PLUM PUDDING · MINCE PIES

CAVIARE ANTARCTIC

CRYSTALLISED FRUITS · CHOCOLATE BONBONS

BUTTER BONBONS · WALNUT · TOFFEE

ALMONDS & RAISINS

WINES

SHERRY · CHAMPAGNE · BRANDY PUNCH · LIQUEUR

CIGARS · CIGARETTES & TOBACCO

SNAPDRAGON

PINE-APPLE CUSTARD · RASPBERRY JELLIES

BUSZARD'S CAKE

GOD SAVE THE KING.

'They looked more weather-worn than anyone I have yet seen. Their faces were scarred and wrinkled, their eyes dull, their hands whitened and creased with the constant exposure.' They had brought back three eggs, to which in the end the Natural History Museum could give only a lukewarm welcome. Scott, however, found the journey through 'the most dismal cold and the fiercest gales in darkness' nothing less than 'heroic'.

On 25 August the sun reappeared. The long night was over and the fateful summer season, the season which they all knew

Midwinter Day celebrations 1911.
OPPOSITE Dinner menu, as it appeared in the new edition of *The South Polar Times*, brought out by Cherry-Garrard the same day.
ABOVE The flag-decorated hut with Scott at the table head, the debris of the meal before them.

The weary, weather-scarred Wilson, Bowers and Cherry-Garrard eating their first hot meal on their return to winter quarters after a 36-day sledge journey of which Cherry-Garrard declared. 'No words can express its horror.'

would see the race to the Pole won or lost, had begun. By mid-September Scott's plans for his journey were complete: 'The scheme seems to have earned full confidence', he wrote; 'it remains to play the game out.' But almost at the same time his wife was writing in her diary, 'I woke up having had a bad dream about you, and then Peter came very close to me and said emphatically: "Daddy won't come back", as though in answer to my silly thoughts.'

During the last fortnight in September Scott took a party for 'a remarkably pleasant and instructive little spring journey', and as a result began to feel more optimistic. Trouble with the ponies, with injured men, with the motor sledges, brought him back nearer to that almost Oriental fatalism which he seems to have felt so often. Yet some of that feeling came from his ability to assess realistically what his prospects were. It was sheer doggedness rather than unthinking enthusiasm which saw him through the difficulties which faced him. He wrote to his wife of Amundsen's chances, 'If he gets to the Pole, it must be before we do, as he is bound to travel fast with dogs and pretty certain to start early. . . . Any attempt to race must have wrecked my plan, besides which it doesn't appear the sort of thing one is out for. . . . In any case you can rely on my not doing or saying anything foolish – only I'm afraid you must be prepared for the chance of finding our venture much belittled.' (On the day he wrote that Amundsen was already three days out from base, feeling his way with the greatest caution through an area criss-crossed by invisible and almost bottomless crevasses.)

Scott wrote a seventeen-page letter to his wife; he spoke of his lack of mental and physical fitness before he arrived in Antarctica.

The root of the trouble was that I had lost confidence in myself. I don't know if it was noticed by others consciously, but it was acted on unconsciously. . . . Had I been what I am now, many things would have been avoided. . . . It seems a woeful long time since I saw your face and there is the likelihood of a woefuller time ahead, and then what? I want to come back having done something, but work here is horribly uncertain and now of course there is the chance of another man setting ahead. . . .

On 31 October Scott wrote to Admiral Sir George Egerton who had strongly supported him as leader of the expedition, 'This is our last night in our very comfortable hut. . . . The motors left some days ago and we saw them disappear over the surface of the Barrier, one twenty miles away going strong. They may not get very far ... but they have already justified their existence. ... We start with the ponies tomorrow.' The advance party, motorised but ponderous, had got away on 24 October; Scott's misgivings about them were soon to be justified, and by 1 November Lashly was writing in his usual dry way, 'Passed Corner Camp and broke another crank head brass so this is an end to the motors. Now comes the man-hauling part of the show.' Some forty miles behind him, Scott had written the last sentence of his Cape Evans diaries: 'The future is in the lap of the gods; I can think of nothing left undone to deserve success.' (Away to the east Amundsen was beyond 81°s and meeting some of the lowest temperatures he would face, down to $-30\,^{\circ}\text{F}$; on 1 November he 'crossed the last crevasse for a long time to come. ... The surface looked grand ahead of us. ...')

That day Scott led his own party out, leaving Cape Evans at eleven in the morning: Wilson, Oates, Bowers, Atkinson, Cherry-Garrard and Wright, with Petty Officers Crean, Evans and Keohane; ten ponies, twenty-three dogs. Ahead of them Lieutenant Evans led Day, Lashly and Hooper as they heaved at the traces of their overloaded sledges, laying a trail of depots, food and fuel for men, fodder for animals. By 9 November this advance party had reached One Ton Depot, while behind them Scott, at Camp 6, was writing, 'Things look hopeful. The weather is beautiful. ...' The next day, however, was a 'very horrid march'; the 11th meant crossing *sastrugi*, those endless, viciously knife-edged ripples which could cover mile after mile; the 13th was 'another horrid march in a terrible light, surface very bad'.

On 15 November the advance party built a camp and a cairn (called Mount Hooper after the youngest of them), but by the 17th Evans was becoming impatient for Scott's arrival. The main party was moving forward some fourteen miles, still forty miles to the north. In London Kathleen Scott was lunching with H.G.Wells – according to her 'a disgusting little bounder' though clever and amusing – and Nansen, who had become a devoted friend, even an admirer; some ten days later he wrote to her, 'It is nice to know there is a woman so like what one has dreamt of but never met.' (Far to the south-east of Scott, Amundsen was toiling up the Axel Heiberg Glacier.)

On 21 November Scott at last reached Evans and his waiting

party. Day told the new arrivals, laughing, 'We haven't seen anything of Amundsen.' But the Norwegians, now on the polar plateau, had stopped at a site they named The Butcher's Shop. They had taken extra dogs to help them up to the 11,000 feet where they now were; here they killed these to feed themselves and the remaining dogs during the rest of the journey. To the British party – itself quite happy to eat their ponies – this seemed abhorrent, and they thought of Amundsen as cold-blooded to have planned such a thing. But Amundsen felt these killings keenly, yet steeled himself in a way Scott would perhaps have found difficult – 'We had agreed to shrink from nothing in order to reach our goal. . . . Shot now followed upon shot – they had an uncanny sound over the great plain. A trusty servant lost his life each time.' Amundsen's position was now 85°30′s; Scott's was almost exactly five degrees latitude further north. Had either party known it, the race was already as good as over.

Scott now sent Day and Hooper back to Cape Evans and reorganised the southward drive. Lieutenant Evans with Atkinson, Wright and Lashly was to keep moving some fifteen miles ahead of the main party, marking out the route and selecting the camp sites. Every sixty-five miles depots were to be left for those returning. Marches were to be at 'night', the main body moving with the ponies, the dog teams following some way in the rear. But the advance party seems never to have got sufficiently ahead to do its work with any ease. And before the end of the month, the weather deteriorated. On the 28th Scott was writing, 'Thick as a hedge, snow falling and drifting with keen southerly wind. . . . When will the wretched blizzard be over?' Cherry-Garrard points out, 'It is curious to see how depressed all our diaries become when this bad weather obtained, and how quickly we must have cheered up whenever the sun came out.' By the 30th Scott could write, 'A very pleasant day for marching', although the ponies were beginning to fail and the first of them had already been killed; on 2 December he recorded, 'We have all taken to horse meat and are so well fed that hunger isn't thought of.' (Amundsen, at 86°47′s, spent the day tent-bound by bad weather – 'the south-easter howls, and the snow beats against the tent'.)

'Our luck in weather is preposterous', Scott wrote on 3 December. 'I roused the hands at 2.30 am . . . by 4.30 it was blowing a full gale from the south. The pony wall fell down, huge drifts collected, and the sledges were quickly buried. It

166

was the strongest wind I have known here in summer.' Two days later he was writing, 'We awoke this morning to a raging, howling blizzard'; they had been travelling within sight of triple-peaked Mount Markham and the other heights of the curving Victoria Land mountains, sign of the continent's true coastline, but now Scott noted that 'one cannot see the next tent, let alone the land.' He wondered if they were 'merely the victims of exceptional local conditions'. If so, there was 'food for thought in picturing our small party struggling against

Bernard Day and Stewart Hooper with two invalid dogs, returning to winter quarters at Cape Evans after a strenuous journey over the Great Ice Barrier.

167

OPPOSITE Captain Roald Amundsen with his dog sledge standing beside the Norwegian flag that marked the first arrival of man at the South Pole on 14 December 1911.

BELOW A full day's rations for one man on sledging journeys.

adversity in one place whilst others go smilingly forward in sunshine'. (Amundsen reported a gale from the north – 'the whole plain was a mass of drifting snow' – yet could add, 'In spite of all hindrances, and of being able to see nothing, the sledge-meters showed nearly twenty-five miles.')

On 6 December Scott wrote, 'Miserable, utterly miserable. . . . The tempest rages with unabated violence. . . . Oh! but this is too crushing, and we are only 12 miles from the Glacier. A hopeless feeling descends on one and is hard to fight off.' (Amundsen: 'December 6 brought the same weather: thick snow, sky and plain all one, nothing to be seen. Nevertheless we made splendid progress.') On the 7th Scott was writing, 'The storm continues and the situation is now serious. . . . We have this morning started our Summit Rations – that is to say, the food calculated from the Glacier Depot has been begun.' (Amundsen on the same day, the sky clearing – 'the feeling was something like that one has on waking from a good nap' – reached a new 'furthest south', beating the earlier Shackleton record.) On 8 December Scott began to dig out the sledges as the weather seemed to improve – but, 'Alas! as I write the

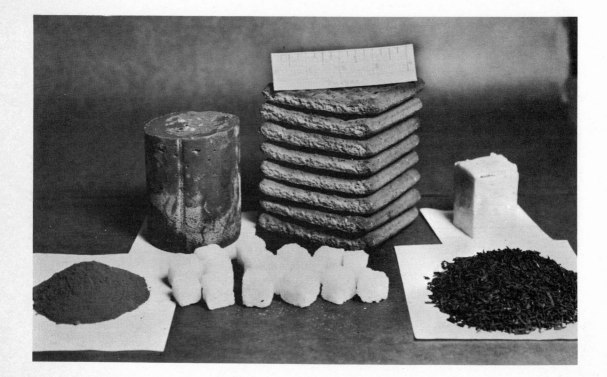

sun has disappeared and snow is again falling. Our case is growing desperate.' By the late evening, however, he was able to add, 'Everything looks more hopeful tonight, but nothing can recall four lost days.'

The next day they moved forward again but by the evening the remaining ponies were utterly exhausted. Although he was well short of where he had hoped to do so, Scott had to order the shooting of these animals. He wrote, 'Poor beasts! they have done wonderfully well . . . it is hard to have to kill them so early.' Cherry-Garrard tells us, 'It was a horrid business, and the place was known as Shambles Camp'; Evans calls it 'the slaughter of the innocents' – only the direct Lashly puts it simply: 'They had their last feed this morning. All killed tonight.'

From now on it was to be mainly man-hauling. On 11 December Meares and the Russian dog expert, Dimitri, having hauled supplies to Lower Glacier Depot, turned once more for the north. (Amundsen reached 89°15′s on that day and could report, 'The snow surface was loose, but ski and sledges glided over it well.') On the 12th Scott notes that the sledges 'got bogged again and again'; on the 13th, 'A most *damnably* dismal day. . . . I suppose we have advanced a bare 4 miles. . . .' But on the 14th he is able to write, 'It is splendid to be getting along and to find some adequate return for the work we are putting into the business.' To the south of him, however, another man had taken the last strides which would ensure that this return would in the end be far less than Scott had hoped.

Amundsen writes:

At three in the afternoon a simultaneous 'Halt!' rang out from the drivers. They had carefully examined their sledge meters, and they all showed the full distance – the Pole by reckoning. The goal was reached, the journey ended. . . . After we had halted we collected and congratulated each other. . . . After this we proceeded to the greatest and most solemn act of the whole journey – the planting of our flag. . . . Five weather-beaten, frost-bitten fists they were that grasped the pole, raised the waving flag in the air, and planted it as the first at the geographical South Pole.

On the 15th Scott, still struggling up the Beardmore Glacier, was held back by renewed snow – 'Our luck is very bad' – but the next day managed eleven miles. On the 17th his party again did well, although Wilson now had bad snow-blindness. At the Pole Amundsen and his four companions, having made

their observations and set up a tent as a precise marker, were at the start of their return journey.

The next few days saw Scott and his companions thrusting forward at a good speed; he begins to sound almost cheerful. The others were very conscious that he was turning over in his mind who should be in what was called The Summit Party – the one-sledge group planned to make the final assault on the Pole. Some had to be eliminated at once and by the 20th he had made up his mind. That night Cherry-Garrard wrote in his diary:

This evening has been rather a shock. . . . Scott came up to me and said that he was afraid he had rather a blow for me. Of course I knew what he was going to say, but could hardly grasp that I was going

Camping in deep snow on the Beardmore Glacier.

back – tomorrow night. The returning party is to be Atch (Atkinson), Silas (Wright), Keohane and self. ... I said I hoped I had not disappointed him, and he caught hold of me and said, 'No – No – No'.

Scott was very conscious of the blow his decision was to those whom he ordered to return: 'I dreaded this necessity of choosing – nothing could be more heartrending.' But in the new journal started on 22 December five names appear written on the fly-leaf – 'Ages: Self 43, Wilson 39, Evans (P.O.) 37, Oates 32, Bowers 28.' So it seems that he may already have felt he would be unable to send back Bowers, who had proved so strong and so valuable throughout the expedition. Yet he cannot have decided finally, for on the 31st he allowed Bowers to depot his skis, as did the rest of the support party to save weight. Thus it appears that Lieutenant Evans, Crean and Lashly, although

Atkinson and the returning party setting off, watched by Scott (far left).

themselves uncertain whether they would be allowed to go through to the end, had already been eliminated; they were to be the Final Supporting Party.

The day after the first returning party under Atkinson left proved difficult for those still travelling south in what Scott called 'a confusion of elevations and depressions'; 23 December was worse – Scott records 'the most extraordinary surface – narrow crevasses ran in all directions. . . . We all fell in one after another and sometimes two together.' Nevertheless, they covered fifteen miles and Scott became cautiously optimistic: 'I trust this may prove the turning point in our fortunes for which we have waited so patiently.' Christmas Day saw mild adventure – 'I looked round and found the second sledge halted some way in the rear. . . . It appears that Lashly went down very suddenly, nearly dragging the crew with him. . . . Lashly is 44 today and as hard as nails. His fall has not even disturbed his equanimity.' Lashly himself, who wrote that the crevasse was 'a thing ... about 50 feet deep and 8 feet wide, and 120 feet long' did permit himself the comment, 'Rather a ghastly sight while dangling in one's harness.'

Nevertheless, in the evening out on that monstrous plateau the party celebrated Christmas with what seemed to them an enormous meal – 'I am so replete I can scarcely write', Scott noted. Later, he gives details of the menu: 'We had four courses. The first, pemmican, full whack, with slices of horse meat flavoured with onion and curry powder and thickened with biscuit; then an arrowroot, cocoa and biscuit hoosh sweetened; then a plum pudding; then cocoa with raisins, and finally a dessert of caramels and ginger.'

Two days later he is recording that steering the party was 'very worrying and tiring'. Difficulties with Evans' sledge did not help – 'I have told them plainly that they must wrestle with the trouble and get it right for themselves' – but by the end of the year he felt he was level with Shackleton's schedule, a challenge which at this time seems to have been on his mind more than that of the Norwegians; but this last he may have been trying to keep as far as possible out of his thoughts. After building Three Degree Depot on New Year's Eve he was able the next day, after celebrating the new year with a stick of chocolate, to write, 'Prospects seem to get brighter – only 170 miles to go and plenty of food left.'

Into the year 1912, then, and over the 87th parallel. On 3 January Lashly, laconic to the end, wrote in his diary, 'The Captain told us this morning we should return tomorrow. That is if they can get along with the load, Mr Evans, myself and Crean. Captain Scott, Captain Oates, Dr Wilson, Mr Bowers and Evans, these are the people going to the Pole. Today has been a very cold wind and low drift, but we have done 12 miles.' In this way, meticulous in the titles courtesy insisted on, Lashly put down the bones of his balked hopes. Lieutenant Evans tells us, 'Briefly then it was a disappointment, but not too great to bear'; he had foreseen that after man-hauling almost all the way from Cape Evans he and Lashly at least were very unlikely to be asked to make the final dash. Nevertheless Scott the next day described him when they parted as 'terribly disappointed but has taken it very well and behaved like a man. Poor old

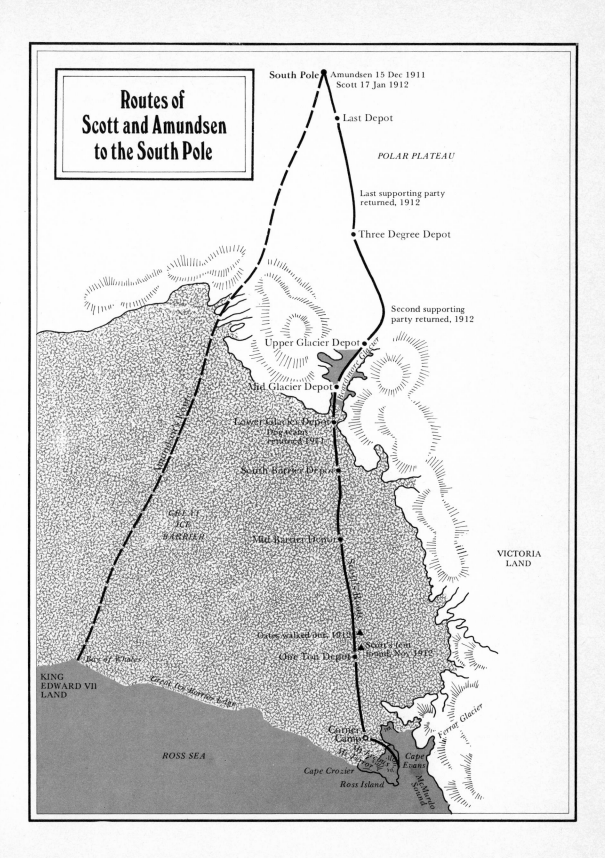

Routes of
Scott and Amundsen
to the South Pole

South Pole • Amundsen 15 Dec 1911
Scott 17 Jan 1912

• Last Depot

POLAR PLATEAU

Last supporting party
returned, 1912

• Three Degree Depot

Second supporting
party returned, 1912

Upper Glacier Depot •

Mid Glacier Depot •

Lower Glacier Depot •
Dog teams
returned 1911

South Barrier Depot •

*GREAT
ICE
BARRIER*

Mid Barrier Depot •

Scott's Route

Oates walked out, 1912 ▲
Scott's tent
▲ found, Nov 1912
One Ton Depot •

Bay of Whales

KING
EDWARD VII
LAND

Great Ice Barrier Edge

*VICTORIA
LAND*

Amundsen's Route

Beardmore Glacier

Ferrar Glacier

Corner
Camp •

Cape Crozier

Ross Island

Cape
Evans

*McMurdo
Sound*

ROSS SEA

Crean wept and even Lashly was affected.' Then Scott looked forward, not without foreboding: 'I wonder what is in store for us. At present everything seems to be going with extraordinary smoothness and one can scarcely believe that obstacles will not present themselves to make our task more difficult.' Almost chidingly, he writes on 5 January, 'What lots of things we think of on these monotonous marches! What castles one builds now hopefully that the Pole is ours.'

The party of five, four of them on skis for most of the time, but Bowers always stumping energetically along on short, muscular legs, were now high on the polar plateau. The ice ridges of *sastrugi* again and again held them up as they struggled southwards, past Shackleton's most southerly camp. (Scott writes, 'We ... I suppose, have made the most southerly camp', a strange note of doubt in what ought to have been a simple observation; was he thinking of Amundsen?) At over ten thousand feet, in a bleak landscape where snow alternated with knife-edged ice and the wind never stopped its long moaning, they moved stubbornly forward, determined to make each day's mileage into double figures, counting the distance yet to go as it diminished, hopeful about, then dreading the outcome, bent over the traces of their sledge, heroic in a struggle they did not yet know they had lost.

Scott took the time to record his admiration for his companions – Wilson, who acted as doctor and as cook, and was 'tough as steel on the traces'; 'Evans, a giant worker with a remarkable headpiece' (although already with the hand injury which may later have helped to cost him his life); 'Little Bowers remains a marvel'; Oates 'goes the whole time'. On 10 January Scott wrote that they were moving on with only eighteen days' food, having left the rest in depots for their return. He was realistic about what faced them: 'Only 85 miles from the Pole, but it's going to be a stiff pull *both ways* apparently. . . .' The next day he was proved right: 'I never had such pulling; all the time the sledge rasps and creaks. We have covered 6 miles, but at fearful cost to ourselves.' It is clear that he was conscious of the way their physical reserves were running out. The next day he makes the point again: 'Another hard grind. . . . About 74 miles from the Pole – can we keep this up for seven days? . . . None of us ever had such hard work before.' Man-hauling at around $-15\,°F$, at an altitude of over ten thousand feet, across rough ice or soft, deep snow, often in the teeth of a force four wind, we

OPPOSITE Wilson watercolour showing open leads in new ice and Mount Discovery in the background.

176

might expect him perhaps to have had doubts about his decisions; to wonder if he had chosen the best team or the best method; to think of other combinations of men which might have given him more power, more steadfastness. Did he ever regret that he had not planned to use dogs to the full? At the time such considerations could not be allowed, decisions had to be taken and adhered to. But had he come to planning another journey there can be no doubt that his experiences would have brought such thoughts to the fore.

On 12 January he was writing, 'It is an effort to keep up the double figures, but if we can do so for another four marches we ought to get through. It is going to be a close thing.' Later he adds, 'We ought to do the trick, but oh! for a better surface.' The next day, over the unyielding, granular snow, they managed another eleven miles – 'The chance holds. . . . Only 51 miles from the Pole tonight. If we don't get to it we shall be damned close.' The following day the weather began to look ominous, and Scott falls again into that exclamatory style which seems to say so much about his anxiety – 'Oh! for a few fine days! So close it seems and only the weather to baulk us.' But by Monday, 15 January the weather had cleared, although the temperature was very low. This meant as always that the surface would become less and less easy for the sledge runners; when they camped at midday, they were all fairly exhausted. Yet by the evening they had covered a total of twelve miles and for the first time Scott seems openly exultant: 'It is wonderful to think that two long marches would land us at the Pole.' It was the last moment left to him for unalloyed optimism.

Tuesday, January 16. The worst has happened, or nearly the worst. . . . About the second hour of the march Bowers' sharp eyes detected what he thought was a cairn; he was uneasy about it, but argued that it must be a *sastrugus*. . . . We marched on, found that it was a black flag tied to a sledge bearer; near by the remains of a camp. . . . This told us the whole story. The Norwegians have forestalled us and are first at the Pole. It is a terrible disappointment, and I am very sorry for my loyal companions. . . . All the day dreams must go; it will be a wearisome return.

The day before, after his moment of optimism, he had seen this moment as an 'appalling possibility'; now it had happened.

The next day saw anticlimax finally confirmed: 'The Pole. Yes, but under very different circumstances from those expected.' The words, THE POLE, were written in capitals, tall,

OPPOSITE Edward Wilson's drawing of the cairn and black flag left by the Norwegians. A day later Scott and his party came to the Pole itself, reached by Amundsen a full month before.

Cairn left by Norwegians - S.SW from Black Flag Camp
Jan. 16. 1912.

Amundsens South Pole mark.   Jan. 18. 1912

but shaky. 'We have had a horrible day', the entry goes on. None of them had slept very much after their shock, then early in the morning had started their final day's run southward. The desolation within them seemed now to envelop the whole world. 'Great God! this is an awful place', Scott wrote, 'and terrible enough for us to have laboured to it without the reward of priority. . . . Now for the run home and a desperate struggle to get the news through first. I wonder if we can do it.'

On 18 January they made the most precise observations they could and calculated what seemed to them the exact location of the Pole. They thought themselves three and a half miles from the exact spot; in the indicated direction they found Amundsen's tent, with the names of the five men who had been there a month before, the Norwegian flag flying, and a letter to be forwarded for King Haakon. This last, it seemed, offended Scott, who did not realise Amundsen had left it in case anything happened to his own party during their northward march (although in fact Amundsen on this day was rapidly approaching the 81st parallel in what he described in his diary as 'unusually fine weather'). Photographs were taken, Wilson made his swift, skilful sketches. They constructed a cairn and 'put up our poor, slighted Union Jack' – a flag Queen Alexandra had given them in the hopeful days before *Terra Nova* first set sail. Scott showed some of his bitterness at the Norwegians in a comment he put in his diary: 'I think it quite evident they aimed to forestall a date quoted by me in London as ideal, *viz* Dec. 22nd.' He still had some kind of hope – that by getting 'the news through first' he might salvage some respect, some part-aged shred of fame; and in this hope he might have been encouraged by the fact that Amundsen, in leaving his letter for Scott to deliver, seems himself to have felt some uncertainty about his return journey. Yet Scott must have known that this hope was faint, with Amundsen already a month gone. His last sentence in that day's entry was more realistic: 'Well, we have turned our back now on the goal of our ambition and must face our 800 miles of solid dragging – and good-bye to most of the day-dreams.'

Since Sir Clements Markham had selected and inspired him thirteen years before, Scott's most urgent ambition had been to become the first human to stand at the South Pole. Now by the cruellest margin, he had been deprived of his moment, so valueless in itself, so monumental in its symbolism. His leadership

Exhausted, their hopes
dashed, Oates, Bowers,
Scott, Wilson and Evans
stand at the South Pole.

was, he felt, an implicit promise of success made to those
who trusted in it (almost his first thought had been, 'I am very
sorry for my loyal companions'). Now that tremendous effort,
the very pain of which seemed to demand its reward, had turned
out to be worthless; that unspoken but solemn promise had
after all been broken. One knows the events, the disasters, of the
return journey, one sees unfolded that long spectacle of courage
and frustration. Yet one is almost forced to wonder what died
in Scott when on that bleak Thursday in 1912 he turned away
from the place which had become a demonstration of his
destroyed hopes, his suddenly devalued life. How much did

he dread the return now, the explanations of a second-best, the oblivion which faces a loser? He was to struggle, he was to fight for his survival – yet he died as though at peace, his concern for others very much alive, his hope for himself gone and hardly, so it seems, regretted.

With the wind helping them and a sail occasionally set to take the best advantage of it, the first days of the return passed in dogged perseverance rather than abrupt adventure. Scott shows his concern for his companions as early as the 20th: 'Bowers . . . must find these long marches very trying with short legs. . . . Oates is feeling the cold and fatigue more than most of us.' On the 23rd Evans showed signs of frost-bite on his face – 'There is no doubt that Evans is a good deal run down. . . . He is very much annoyed with himself, which is not a good sign.' By the next day Scott is commenting, 'Things beginning to look a little

Amundsen's tent at the South Pole with Scott, Oates, Wilson and Evans beside it.

serious. A strong wind at the start has developed into a full blizzard at lunch. . . . This is the second full gale since we left the Pole. I don't like the look of it. Is the weather breaking up? If so, God help us, with the tremendous summit journey and scant food.'

They followed their own outward tracks, in the process picking up, among other objects, Oates' pipe, dropped on the southward journey. Towards the end of January, they were travelling nearly twenty miles a day, and Scott's entries begin to sound almost placid, except when he refers to the health of the party. Wilson, still afflicted with partial snow-blindness, damaged a tendon in his leg. Scott himself fell early in February, hurting his right shoulder. All the time, Evans' sufferings grew worse; on 30 January he 'dislodged two finger-nails', by 4 February, having fallen twice, he is being described as 'rather dull and incapable', probably from concussion. By then Wilson's leg had improved but Scott knew very well that the worst of the journey still lay ahead, among the ice and crevasses of the Beardmore Glacier, and on the Barrier surface beyond.

On 7 February they reached Upper Glacier Depot, finding a note from Lieutenant Evans to say he had passed there safely three weeks earlier. The day before Scott had been more worried than ever about Petty Officer Evans, 'the chief anxiety now . . . he shows considerable signs of being played out'. Now, while remarking 'most of us are fit', he added that Evans was 'going steadily downhill'. Nevertheless, they moved on north-ward, down from the high plateau – 'the relief of being out of the wind and in a warmer temperature is inexpressible', Scott recorded. Evans kept up with the party as, scientists in spirit still, they examined rock falls, quartzites, pieces of coal holding fast the impression of leaves and stalks which had been dead for millennia. 'A lot could be written on the delight of setting foot on rock after 14 weeks of snow and ice', Scott remarked.

Snow began to fall lightly on the 10th; on the 11th the surface became more difficult than anything they had had to face before. Scott called it 'the worst day we have had during the trip' and talks of 'the worst ice mess I have ever been in. For three hours we plunged on on ski, first thinking we were too much to the right, then too much to the left; meanwhile the disturb-ance got worse and my spirits received a very rude shock. There were times when it seemed impossible to find a way out. . . .' He describes this 'irregular crevassed surface giving way to huge chasms, closely packed and most difficult to cross'. As a result Scott was unsure how far he was from the next depot, nor whether they were still on precisely the right route; he ordered a reduction in rations. On the 12th he again writes of the party as 'tired and despondent, arrived in a horrid maze of crevasses and fissures. Divided councils caused our course to be erratic after this' – a note which carries a suggestion of argument, of disagreement, perhaps of some loss of confidence in himself, some loss of morale in the group as a whole. A little desperately now he writes, 'We *must* get there tomorrow.'

And on the morrow, the 13th, they did in fact reach Mid Glacier Depot, again finding to their relief that the other parties had passed safely through. But Scott remained worried about his companions: both Bowers and Wilson had been badly hit by snow-blindness and 'Evans has no power to assist with camping work.' A good day followed, and another, although Scott again notes that they are getting short of food. On 16 February he records that 'Evans has nearly broken down in brain, we think' and that 'the weather is all against us'. It was snowing again, and he tells himself, a little bleakly, that 'it's no use meeting trouble half way'. In truth, trouble had already come more than half way to meet him.

The entry for 17 February begins starkly, 'A very terrible day'. Again and again Evans fell behind; again and again the party stopped, and then once more were forced to forge ahead. At the lunch break, however, Evans did not appear at all; looking back, they saw him at some distance. They skied back to him. 'I was the first to reach the poor man and shocked at his appearance; he was on his knees with clothing disarranged, hands uncovered and frostbitten, and a wild look in his eyes.' They tried to move him, but after a few strides he fell again. 'Wilson, Bowers, and I went back for the sledge, whilst Oates remained with him. When we returned he was practically unconscious, and when we got him into the tent quite comatose. He died quietly at 12.30 am.'

The next day they reached Shambles Camp where, since there was plenty of horse meat, they 'had a fine supper'. Scott, however, was still anxious about the surfaces that waited for them on the Barrier itself. (At home his wife was writing in her diary, 'I was very taken up with you all evening. I wonder if anything special is happening to you.') On 19 February they 'struggled out 4.6 miles in a short day over a really terrible

ABOVE and OPPOSITE Kathleen Scott in her
artist's studio with her son Peter, now better
known as Sir Peter Scott of the Wildfowl Trust.

186

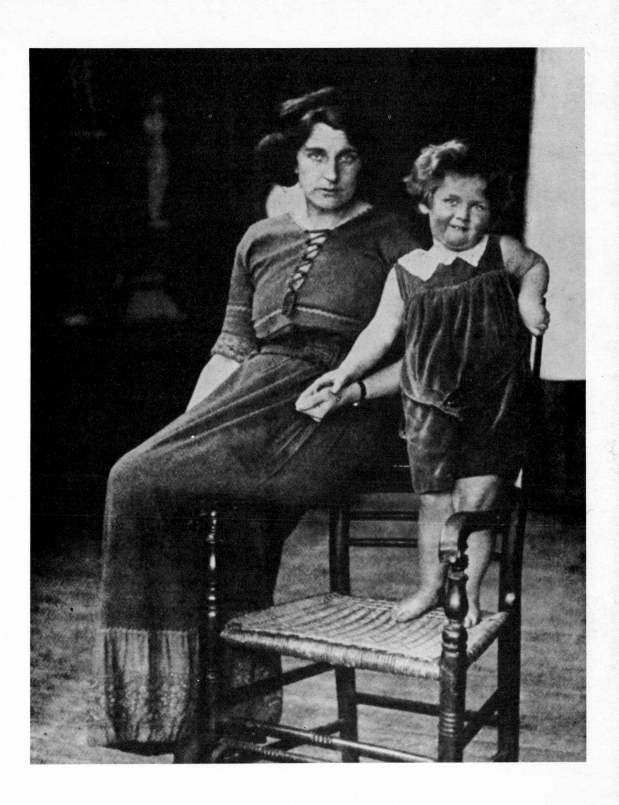

187

surface – it has been like pulling over desert sand. . . .', and Scott ends the day's entry with the words, 'I wonder what is in store for us, with some little alarm at the lateness of the season.'

The 20th brought the same difficulties – 'Terribly slow progress', Scott records. On the 21st, the march was 'almost as bad as yesterday. . . . We never won a march of $8\frac{1}{2}$ miles with greater difficulty, but we can't go on like this', and on the 22nd he says 'There is little doubt we are in for a rotten critical time going home.' But that evening they ate their pony stew – their 'hoosh' – and Scott more hopefully points out that after such a meal 'one feels really strong and vigorous again'. The optimism continued through the next day, although they covered less than nine miles, and through the 24th, when they reached the next depot and could renew their supplies – with the exception of oil, the strange shortage of which Scott refers to several times and which has never been properly explained. (Seepage and evaporation are the most likely causes, probably because the leather washers under the bung had begun to perish; Scott, however, perhaps because of his state of mind, seems to have suspected negligence or selfishness on the part of the others who had made use of the depots.) Later that day, Scott writes, 'a little despondent again' and it is clear that he is now in a constant state of anxiety about his party's survival.

The temperatures were again beginning to drop; Scott felt that the season was closing in early and that he was in a race against it, as he was in combat against distance, weather and surface conditions. By the 27th his diary records a night minimum temperature of $-37\,°$F. The whole party was now beginning to weaken and this day saw Wilson's last entry in his own journal, a sign that even his morale and energy were being undermined. The following night, the temperature fell again, to $-40\,°$F. By 2 March, however, they had struggled through to Mid Barrier Depot. In the daily entries which Scott still meticulously kept, he writes that 'we have suffered three distinct blows which have placed us in a bad position. First we found a shortage of oil. . . . Second, Titus Oates disclosed his feet, the toes showing very bad indeed. . . . The third blow came in the night, when the wind, which we had hailed with some joy, brought dark, overcast weather.'

The temperatures were now lower than ever, and it took them an hour-and-a-half to put on their footgear in the mornings. The shortage of fuel was therefore of the greatest concern,

OPPOSITE ABOVE Ice front near Kainan Bay.
BELOW Pancake ice in the Ross Sea.

for in the gathering cold, hot meals provided a prime source of energy and, psychologically, always offered a sense of well-being, however temporary. It also meant that it limited the time they could allow themselves to cover the seventy-one miles to the next depot, since they would have to do so before their oil ran out. Yet that day they did less than ten miles, and the next morning travelled four-and-a-half hours for the same number of miles across a surface which even more than usually resisted the sledge runners. 'God help us', Scott wrote, 'we can't keep up this pulling, that is certain. Amongst ourselves we are unendingly cheerful, but what each man feels in his heart I can only guess. . . .'

Next day, 4 March, he writes, 'Things looking *very* black indeed.' They were over forty miles now from the next depot, with a week's food but only three or four days' supply of fuel. None of them was as yet openly despondent, but 'one's heart sinks as the sledge stops dead at some *sastrugi* behind which the surface sand lies thickly heaped'. He feared the return of colder weather, for he realised that Oates would not easily be able to stand it. Thinking ahead to the next depot, he allows himself the question, 'Shall we get there?', a sign that he was putting the appalling alternatives squarely before himself.

By 5 March Oates' feet were in a very bad condition, one very swollen, while Wilson was feeling the increasing cold more than the rest. Despite the efforts they were making, none of them could now stay warm and the wind seemed to cut through their outer garments. Perhaps the lack of food, the collapse of hope, their long continued loss of weight, made them more vulnerable now to these dropping temperatures. Yet Scott records, 'We mean to see the game through with a proper spirit. . . . One can only say "God help us!" and plod on our weary way, cold and very miserable, though outwardly cheerful.' Yet the next day their cheerfulness was tried; snow fell and they lost their way, since their own outward tracks which they were still following had become obscured. Worse than this, Oates could give them only intermittent help. 'He makes no complaint, but his spirits only come up in spurts now. . . .' Almost despairingly, Scott looks back to the '9-mile days' which at the time he had thought such slow progress.

On 8 March a curious, even cruel, news item appeared in the British newspapers. As *The Times* reported from Wellington, New Zealand, 'A rumour, which however lacks confirmation,

OPPOSITE Captain Oates, a 'gallant gentleman' who sacrificed himself to save his companions.

is current here that 'Captain Amundsen states that Captain Scott has reached the South Pole. . . . On inquiry at Mrs Scott's house, the following information was given: – "There is no news from Captain Scott. The news reported in the evening papers does not even purport to come from Captain Amundsen, even if he could have obtained it" . . .' In the Antarctic, Scott and his companions, themselves gripped by a less subtle cruelty, were a day's march from the depot at Mount Hooper. Wilson's feet were continuing to give trouble, while 'poor Oates' left foot can never last out'.

On Saturday, 9 March, London discovered the truth of what had happened at the Pole, of who had stood there first. Tepidly *The Times* rallied its readers to the praise of Amundsen: 'Whatever we may think of the way he went about it, we are bound to congratulate him on his success.' In a leader the newspaper admits, 'There is no need to pretend that we should not have been glad to see the most conspicuous triumph in Antarctic exploration secured by the British expedition.' Then, for a while, it whistles to keep up its spirits, suggesting that since no one knew what Scott had been doing nor where he was, he might even have reached the Pole before the Norwegians. It attacks Amundsen's sportsmanship, and his apparently abrupt decision to make for the South Pole instead of the North: 'This sudden change of plan and the unnecessary secrecy which surrounded it were felt to be not quite in accordance with the spirit of fair and open competition which had hitherto marked Antarctic exploration.' Expeditions to far-away places, they seemed to feel, were an extension of a code which only bounders and foreigners ignored. Members of the Royal Geographical Society were scant in their applause when their President announced he had sent Amundsen their congratulations. Only Kathleen Scott understood that a whole future had tumbled, that what was outrage in London would be tragedy and despair in the Antarctic itself. 'I worked badly and my head rocked. I'm not going to recount what I have been feeling.'

Camped beyond Mount Hooper on 10 March the weakening Oates asked Wilson whether he would survive the journey, although Scott thought that he 'must know that he can never get through'. At the same time it was clear that Oates was holding them up, being so slow to get started after breakfast and lunch that the effects of the meal had begun to wear off before the party could get under way. Yet Scott retained compassion:

OPPOSITE ABOVE Nimrod Glacier.
BELOW Frozen lake surrounded by pinnacled ice.

'Poor chap! it is too pathetic to watch him; one cannot but try to cheer him up.' They had replenished their supplies at the Mount Hooper Depot and should have felt more secure. Instead, Scott recorded, 'Cold comfort. Shortage on our allowance all round.' He had been hoping against hope that dog teams would have met him there, as had been partly planned.

The dogs had in fact been waiting at One Ton Depot with Cherry-Garrard and Dimitri. They had been there since 3 March, held fast by blinding head winds and by a shortage of dog food. Rather than take the risk of going farther south and discovering not only that the dogs had run short of food but also that in the bad conditions he had missed Scott's party, Cherry-Garrard remained where he was for six whole days. Scott, after all, would have to come to One Ton Depot. And Cherry-Garrard knew that enough supplies had been left in the depots farther south to keep Scott and his companions going. 'Thus I felt little anxiety for the Polar Party', he writes. 'But I was getting anxious about my companion . . . it was clear that Dimitri was feeling the cold.' The temperatures, as the men returning from the Pole had found, were abnormally low and Dimitri was able to do less and less with his right hand. His side was also badly affected. Calculating that they needed eight days' food to get back, Cherry-Garrard knew that he had to start back on this same day (10 March), the day that Scott marched beyond the depot at Mount Hooper: 'Getting our gear together, and the dogs more or less in order after their six days was cold work, and we started in minus thirties and a head wind.' Thus Cherry-Garrard, turning to the north and safety, conscious of having left the supplies which, he was certain, would see Scott and the others through to Bluff Depot, Corner Camp and Hut Point.

There was no way for him to know that some sixty miles to the south, Scott at that moment was already well aware that things were going 'steadily downhill'. If Oates went under, he doubted if they would be able to get through – 'With great care we might have a dog's chance, but no more.' They had travelled for no more than half-an-hour before the conditions had forced them to stop: 'We . . . are spending the rest of the day in a comfortless blizzard camp, wind quite foul.'

The next day Oates, conscious of holding back the others, began fairly calmly to ask what he should do; it was clear to

Scott that he was thinking of self-sacrifice and there is a strong underlying sense in what he writes that he felt Oates would be performing the right, stoical action if he were to do so; 'he is a brave fine fellow and understands the situation'. Certainly Ponting, the photographer, later wrote that just before the polar journey had begun Oates had said categorically that for anyone who broke down and became a hindrance to the others there was only one course open and that was self-sacrifice; so clear was he about this, that he felt there should be a revolver available for this precise purpose. It is likely that on those long marches and lonely camps he and the others had already discussed this and come to some conclusions. In any case, the solution at which Oates was now hinting seems to have led Scott to realise that they were very near the time when suicide might be the only way out for any of them. 'I practically ordered Wilson to hand over the means of ending our troubles. . . . Wilson had no choice between doing so and our ransacking the medicine case. We have 30 opium tabloids apiece and he is left with a tube of morphine.' Scott knew there was a strong chance they would be needed; calculating ahead, he considered what daily mileage they could attain and what they needed to attain in order to cover the fifty-five miles to One Ton Depot before their food ran out. The difference, his sums told him, was thirteen miles – two days' march at their present rate of progress, 'even if things get no worse'.

Two days later, having covered only another twelve miles, he wrote, 'No doubt about the going downhill, but everything going wrong for us.' They moved on, for once with the wind behind them and the sail set, but after a while the wind shifted. The midday temperature was $-43\,°$F. Only Scott and Bowers were now really active and even for them making camp was a long, laborious process; the tent, too, no longer gave them any true respite, for the cold never left them for an instant. 'It must be near the end, but a pretty merciful end. . . . No idea there could be temperatures like this at this time of year with such winds. Truly awful outside the tent. Must fight it out to the last biscuit, but can't reduce rations.' Still calculating, still aware, understanding fully his predicament, one sees him lying in the cramped tent, his drawn face, bearded now, seamed and cracked by the weather, bent over the little notebook, his mittened hand perhaps most laboriously keeping these daily, desperate entries which he must have known might never even be read – this remarkable record of their moral resilience, their physical collapse.

The next entry, however, shows that for him too the world was becoming a blur of effort and pain. For the first time, having missed a couple of days, he is not sure of the date; he thinks it is 17 March. On the morning of the 15th Oates had said he could no longer go on and asked to be left in his sleeping bag, but the others would not abandon him. He struggled on and was still with them as they made camp.

We can testify to his bravery. He has borne intense suffering for weeks without complaint. . . . He did not – would not – give up hope till the very end. He was a brave soul. This was the end. He slept through the night before last, hoping not to wake; but he woke in the morning – yesterday. It was blowing a blizzard. He said 'I am just going outside and may be some time'. He went out into the blizzard and we have not seen him since.

The others had tried to stop him but understood his bravery, even his need for a dignified ending of his own choice. 'We all hope to meet the end with a similar spirit, and assuredly the end is not far off.'

On 18 March, Scott calculated they were twenty-one miles from One Ton Depot. His own right foot was now badly frost-bitten – 'Bowers takes first place in condition, but there is not much to choose after all. The others are still confident of getting through – or pretend to be – I don't know!' Next day they dragged themselves and their sledge – 'dreadfully heavy' this – to within sixteen miles of the depot. 'We have two days' food but barely a day's fuel.' As for his feet, 'amputation is the least I can hope for now, but will the trouble spread?' The temperature was still forty below, the wind almost dead against them. Yet that afternoon, they pushed forward almost another five miles; they were eleven miles from safety.

On Tuesday, 20 March, a blizzard blew all day. They could not move at all. Scott decided that Wilson and Bowers should try and push through to the depot and bring fuel back, but even this 'forlorn hope' failed them. The next entry, for 22 and 23 March, says, 'Blizzard as bad as ever – Wilson and Bowers unable to start – tomorrow last chance – no fuel and only one or two of food left – must be near the end. Have decided it shall be natural – we shall march for the depot with or without our effects and die in our tracks.'

Then there are no more entries for six days, as the blizzard

blew their lives away, hour by hour, day by day. Not after all upright and thrusting forward with the last of their energy, they had to lie, calm, yet feeling their strength ebb, feeling time and the world turn against them. Did Scott remember then that other blizzard which had held them for three days over a year ago, north of the 80th parallel, north of where they lay now; and which had forced them to lay One Ton Depot twenty miles short of its intended place? They had already covered nine of those miles; they would have reached safety on 15 March if the depot had been on that fateful line of latitude. Scott does not mention it; perhaps he was too weary, too weak to rummage through the might-have-beens. On 29 March, he writes again.

Since the 21st we have had a continuous gale from wsw and sw. We had fuel to make two cups of tea apiece and bare food for two days on the 20th. Every day we have been ready to start for our depot *11 miles* away, but outside the door of the tent it remains a scene of whirling drift. I do not think we can hope for any better things now.

Painting by Dollman of Oates, severely frost-bitten, walking into the blizzard to his death. His body was never discovered.

197

Winter Quarters
Oct 26 1911

My dear Smith

When this reaches you I hope that you will have received later news of our welfare than I am now able to give. But your interest in the Expedition is so close that I know you will be eager to have all details and I hope to arrange for you to get pretty full information even if, as is probable, your particular friends do not return in the Terra Nova this ...

Of these particular friends my pen can only give a very inadequate account — it cannot find words to praise the difficulty — ... has been all that you expected of him and I know that is saying a great deal ... I find myself daily wondering at his ...

. . . . And with my very kindest regards believe me yours sincerely

R. Scott

1. IN THE WRITING OF THE DIARY OF "ROUGH NOTES" WHICH TOLD THE TERRIBLE, HEROIC STORY OF THE DEATH OF CAPTAIN SCOTT AND HIS SOUTH POLE PARTY: LAST NEWS OF THE EXPLORER—A LETTER FROM WINTER QUARTERS, OCTOBER 26, 1911.

2. WITH HIS BABY SON, BEFORE THE START FOR THE ILL-FATED EXPEDITION: CAPTAIN SCOTT WITH PETER.

We give the reproduction of the handwriting of Captain Scott which appears on this page that some idea may be gained of the manuscript of the diary found with his body by the search-party. It is part of a letter sent by Captain Scott to Mr. Reginald Smith, of Messrs. Smith, Elder and Co., dated "Winter Quarters, October 26, 1911"; and received in London on May 11, 1912—some six weeks, that is to say, after the explorer's death. As we note elsewhere, Captain Scott's only child, Peter, was born on September 14, 1909. He alone of those near and dear to Captain Scott does not know of his father's fate.

REPRODUCTION OF THE LETTER BY COURTESY OF MR. REGINALD SMITH; PHOTOGRAPH BY COPPERFIELD.

We shall stick it out to the end, but we are getting weaker, of course, and the end cannot be far.

It seems a pity, but I do not think I can write more.

R.Scott

Last Entry: 'For God's sake look after our people.'

The writing straggles at the end, is clumsy with the weakness of the hand that wrote it; but the letters stand upright, the words are legible. And in that period of silence, when the journal tells us nothing of their sufferings, nor of the way in which they adjusted to them, faced their despair, the ending of their lives, and perhaps the value of the causes for which they had risked them, considered what must have seemed to them their failure and the hideous face fortune had shown them since the beginning; in that period, despite the weakness, the lack of food and the terrible, unending cold, Scott wrote his concerned yet almost phlegmatic farewells. He wrote to Wilson's wife and described his friend, 'everlastingly cheerful and ready to sacrifice himself for others, never a word of blame to me for leading him into this mess.... I can do no more to comfort you than to tell you that he died as he lived, a brave, true man.' He wrote to Bowers' mother; he was, he said, finishing his journey 'in company with two gallant, noble gentlemen. One of these is your son. ... As the troubles have thickened his dauntless spirit ever shone brighter. ...' He wrote to J.M.Barrie, attempting now to heal some wound in the other's affection for him, then asking him, a man of fame and influence, to do what he might to get recognition for the claims of the widows and children he and his companions were leaving behind. 'I may not have proved a great explorer', he wrote, 'but we have done the greatest march ever made and come very near to great success.' Later he added a postscript: 'We are very near the end, but have not and will not lose our good cheer. ... We did intend to finish ourselves when things proved like this, but we have decided to die naturally in the track. ... I never met a man in my life whom I admired and loved more than you, but I could never show you how much your friendship meant to me, for you had much to give and I nothing.' He wrote to Kinsey, his agent in New Zealand, to men who had helped sponsor him as leader of the expedition, to his publisher, to his brother-in-law, to old Navy colleagues.

Last came what were probably the most difficult of the letters, those to Kathleen and to his mother. The latter he comforted

OPPOSITE The public interest and sympathy in the fate of Scott and his party was widely reflected in the press who published any snippets of news available. This example shows a letter from Scott to a friend in London and one of the rare photographs of Scott with his baby son.

199

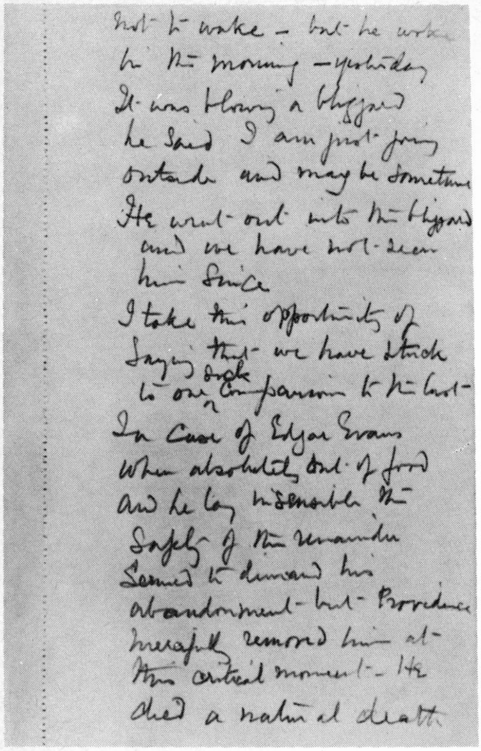

not to wake — but he woke
in the morning — yesterday
It was blowing a blizzard
he said I am just going
outside and may be some time
He went out into the blizzard
and we have not seen
him since
I take this opportunity of
saying that we have stuck
to our sick companions to the last
In case of Edgar Evans
when absolutely out of food
and he lay insensible the
safety of the remainder
seemed to demand his
abandonment but Providence
mercifully removed him at
this critical moment — He
died a natural death

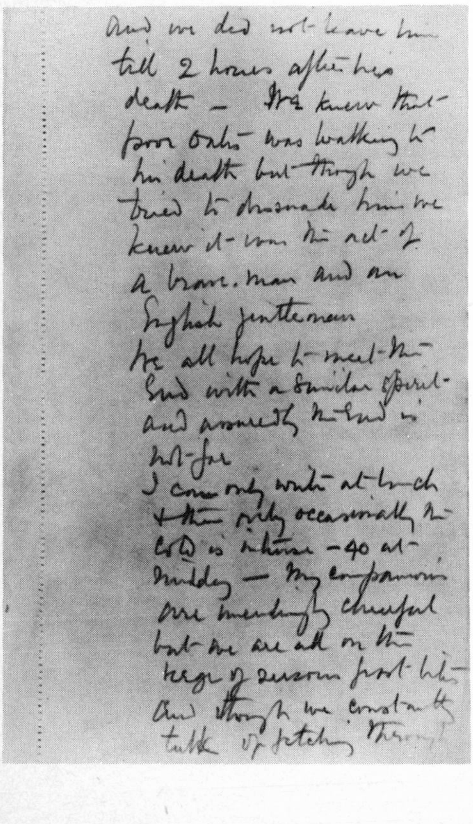

And we did not leave him
till 2 hours after his
death — We knew that
poor Oates was walking to
his death but though we
tried to dissuade him we
knew it was the act of
a brave man and an
English gentleman
We all hope to meet the
end with a similar spirit
and assuredly the end is
not far
I can only write at lunch
+ then only occasionally the
cold is intense — 40 at
midday — My companions
are unendingly cheerful
but we are all on the
verge of serious frost bites
And though we constantly
talk of fetching through

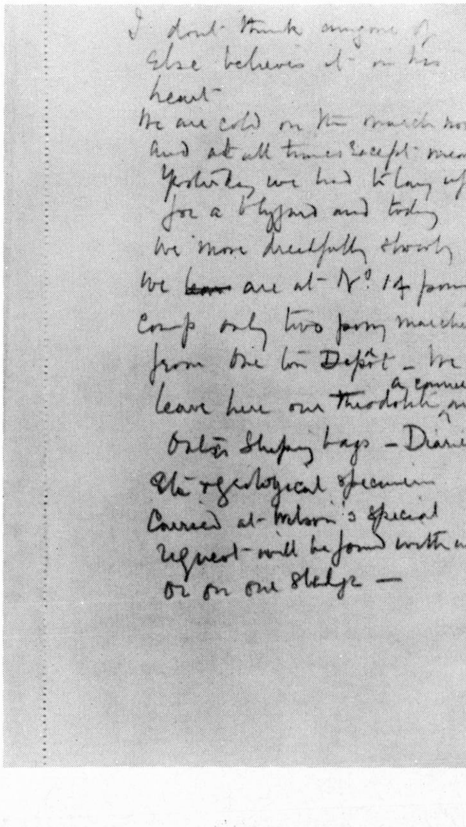

I don't think anyone of
else believes it in his
heart
We are cold on the march now
and at all times except meals
Yesterday we had to lay up
for a blizzard and today
we move dreadfully slowly
We are at No 14 from
camp only two days marches
from the one ton Depôt — We
leave here our theodolite and a compass and
Oates sleeping bags — Diaries
etc & geological specimens
carried at Wilson's special
request will be found with us
or on our sledge —

Extracts from the last
entries to Scott's diary, found
in the tent beside his body.

we shall stick it out
to the end but we
are getting weaker of
course and the end
cannot be far.

It seems a pity but
I do not think I can
write more —

R Scott

Last Entry —

For God's Sake look
after our people

as best he could, assuring her of the strength of what remained to him of religious feeling, reiterating his belief 'that there is a God – a merciful God' and remembering even at this point, perhaps with some guilt, perhaps with satisfaction, how he had faced up to his responsibility for her: 'you will know that you were always very much in my heart and that I strove to put you into more comfortable circumstances.'

His letter to Kathleen was addressed, with that realism which marks everything he wrote about his desperate situation, 'To my Widow'. He assured her that he had suffered no pain, he commended their son to her care and as a source of comfort to her. He urges her to remarry 'when the right man comes to help you in life'. With his usual and seemingly endless diffidence, he tells her, 'I wasn't a very good husband, but I hope I shall be a good memory. Certainly the end is nothing for you to be ashamed of, and I like to think that the boy will have a good start in his parentage of which he may be proud.' His thoughts stray back again and again to their son, but he tells her, 'You just know that quite the worst aspect of this situation is the thought that I shall not see you again.' Then, in a continuation written some time later, 'What lots and lots I could tell you of this journey. How much better it has been than lounging about in too great comfort at home. What tales you would have had for the boy, but oh, what a price to pay. . . .'

Finally, he wrote his MESSAGE TO THE PUBLIC, which begins, 'The causes of the disaster are not due to faulty organisation, but to misfortune in all the risks which had to be undertaken.' He lists the early loss of his ponies, the weather, and the soft snow on the lower slopes of the glacier. He points out what the loss of Edgar Evans, who had been 'thought the strongest man of the party', meant to them; he sets out the extraordinarily low temperatures which they had to face. He writes, 'I do not think human beings ever came through such a month as we have come through', but adds that they might even then have survived if it had not been for the collapse of Oates, 'a shortage of fuel in our depots for which I cannot account, and, finally, but for the storm which has fallen on us within 11 miles of the depot at which we hoped to secure our final supplies. Surely misfortune could scarcely have exceeded this last blow.' He says he does not regret the journey,

... which has shown that Englishmen can endure hardships, help one another, and meet death with as great a fortitude as ever in the past.

We took risks, we knew we took them; things have come out against us, and therefore we have no cause for complaint. . . . These rough notes and our dead bodies must tell the tale, but surely, surely, a great rich country like ours will see that those who are dependent on us are properly provided for.

He signed it; on 29 March he made the last entry in his journal (but perhaps that last scrawled appeal was made even later). It seems probable that Bowers died first, and then Wilson; last of all, Scott, like a leader making all secure before departure. Then there was nothing but the small tent, an incongruity on the white, dead plain, the hard crystals of the flying snow, the groan of the wind; then the long Antarctic night closed over all.

By the beginning of April it became clear to those waiting that Scott and the others had not survived. Cherry-Garrard wrote in his diary, 'We have got to face it now. The Pole Party will not in all probability ever get back. And there is no more we can do.' However, they had to let the winter roll by and the light return before they could begin to send out a search party. It was 12 November when Cherry-Garrard, with the searching dog teams, suddenly saw 'Wright turn away from the course by himself. . . . He had seen what he thought was a cairn, and then something looking black by its side. A vague kind of wonder gradually gave way to real alarm. . . . Wright came across to us. "It is the tent." I do not know how he knew.'

Inside Wilson lay as he had died, quietly, his hands folded on his chest. Bowers, his feet to the door, had also died without pain, probably in sleep. Between the two lay Scott, the flaps of his sleeping bag thrown back. The green wallet which protected his diaries lay under his bag and on the ground-sheet were the letters he had written. His left hand was stretched out, touching his closest friend, Wilson. The tent itself was tidy; near Scott stood an improvised lamp, the light from which had allowed him to write his last messages. A bag of tobacco lay near Scott's head; and elsewhere a bag of tea. They had carried with them to the end all their scientific notes, their measurements and records, thirty-five pounds of geological specimens; all these were found, evidence of an impersonal devotion.

Atkinson recounted Scott's description of the death of Oates and the last entries in that calmly desperate journal. Then he read the burial service. As Cherry-Garrard puts it, 'Perhaps it

The cairns in the desolation
of the Antarctic which mark
the graves of Scott, Wilson
and Bowers.

has never been read in a more magnificent cathedral and under more impressive circumstances – for it is a grave which kings must envy.' They took away the tent-poles and let the canvas cover the three dead men. Over them they built a cairn, with a cross above it made from the pieces of two skis; on either side of the cairn they placed an upright sledge. In a cylinder near the eastern sledge they left a memorial message naming all five of those who had died on that polar journey. Somewhat later, in January, they erected a nine-foot cross on the summit of Observation Hill, high above Hut Point. On it they carved an inscription, a line from Tennyson written on the fly-leaf of Scott's volume of Browning: 'To strive, to seek, to find, and not to yield.'

It was mid-February when Britain and the world learned of Scott's death. On 12 February 1913 *The Times* wrote, 'No more pathetic and tragic story has ever been unfolded than that of the gallant band of Antarctic explorers whose unavailing heroism now fills the public mind with mingled grief and admiration.' It searched for meaning in these deaths, and found it.

This Antarctic Expedition has a value of its own. . . . It is a proof that in an age of depressing materialism men can still be found to face known hardship, heavy risk and even death, in pursuit of an idea, and that the unconquerable will can carry them through, loyal to the last to the charge they have undertaken. That is the temper of men who build empires, and while it lives among us we shall be capable of maintaining the Empire that our fathers builded.

This was no patriotic distortion of Scott's purposes or ideals – these were sentiments of which he would have approved and to which he was committed: it was partly to make people feel this that he had gone south in the first place.

Kathleen was not present at the memorial service which was held in St Paul's Cathedral on 14 February. She was at sea, travelling to New Zealand to meet a man whose widow she had been for almost a year. It was another five days before the captain of the liner, in understandable distress, showed her the message he had received giving the news of her husband's death. She read, she played deck games, she spent sleepless nights on the moonlit upper decks – 'Anything to get that awful, haunting picture out of my head.' As yet she knew very little of what had happened. She wrote, 'All these long, weary days with no more news'; nevertheless, she understood what his

The *Terra Nova* being towed into a London dock in 1913.

diaries prove continued to obsess him to the end, his obligations, his concern for others: 'I think never was there a man with such a sense of responsibility and duty, and the agony of leaving his job undone, losing the other lives, and leaving us uncared for, must have been unspeakable.'

A Memorial Appeal Fund was launched; it began slowly, almost reluctantly, partly because four newspapers opened funds of their own, and people were uncertain what the money would be used for. Once the various appeals had been melded into one and the subscription list headed by the King and Queen, money began to come from all over the country – nearly £30,000 in three days, almost £75,000 altogether. Grants were made, in order of rank – Kathleen, now Lady Scott, allowed to use the title that would have been hers had her husband lived to be knighted, was awarded £8,500. The widow of Petty Officer Evans, with a naval pension of £48 a year to keep herself and her three children, was given £1,250. But such was social justice in post-Edwardian England.

About Scott himself the shell of legend hardened. A score of memorials have gone up to him in various parts of the world, not the least of which was the statue, unveiled in London in 1916, modelled by Kathleen herself. The demands of patriotism shaped his memory; he epitomised the virtues of courage, stoicism, endurance, steadfastness, which the British saw as peculiarly their own. By displaying them, he confirmed their myths, and did so at precisely the moment when their confidence in themselves was beginning to wane. The legend, how-ever, catches that mood too, in its bitter-sweet way – Scott, after all, was in the end a loser. He was second to the Pole, he did not survive the return journey. It was not victory, but courage in adversity, which so captured the British imagination. Would the French, would the Germans, have so rapturously acclaimed a beaten man; would they so long and so freshly have kept him in the national memory?

Legend simplifies its heroes. Under its weight the complexi-ties of an individual are pressed out – a national pantheon is a two-dimensional heaven. Scott has dwindled to become little more than his courage, his sense of responsibility; 'For God's sake look after our people' has echoed down the decades, its nobility self-evident, its concern truly tragic. Yet he was com-plex, a strange man, giving little away. Why did he carry always that central diffidence, that sense of an ultimate

OPPOSITE Commander Evans speaking to Kathleen Scott (centre), following the ceremony at Buckingham Palace where the King presented her with her husband's medal.

208

Scott's base at Cape Evans,
from a recent photograph.
Most of the building is still
in fairly good repair.

unworthiness which seems at times to have driven him on? What were the fits of abstraction which beset him, the absent-mindedness which these gave rise to? And from what part of the soul came the persistent melancholia, the constant sense of death all about, the fatalism?

He was an inward man, his closed face offering little of the secrets within. He was never easily approachable, never a man renowned for bonhomie; he had long periods when he would withdraw, become cool, take back the small intimacies he might have allowed himself. At times, for example, he would call Lieutenant Evans 'Teddy', but only at times – no one knew when it would be 'Evans' again. He had suppressed the bad temper which when he was younger used to flare up almost without warning; his black moods of depression he never conquered. In 1909 he had written to his wife, 'I can't describe what overcomes me. I'm obsessed with the view of life as a struggle for existence, and then forced to see how little past efforts have done to give me a place in the struggle'; she had called this intermittent gloom 'the dread thundercloud'.

One senses in his letters a feeling that he is in some way merely ordinary beside Kathleen's brilliance, and perhaps the brilliance of others – a curious feeling of inadequacy. In the last letter he actually sent her, brought back by Lieutenant Evans from well south of the 87th parallel, he said, 'I think it is going to be all right. . . . So this is simply to say that I love you and that you needn't be ashamed of me, or the boy either. I have led this business – not nominally but actually – so that no man will or can say I wasn't fit to lead through the last lap that is before us.' The note is curiously defensive; there had been argument about his leadership certainly, but why the conviction that he had constantly to prove himself to her, that otherwise she would be 'ashamed' of him? A common enough phrase, perhaps, but one offered at a moment of truth; others at such a time might not have bothered with such self-torture or self-questioning.

It is clear that he was inwardly, almost in secret, sensitive, highly aware, a dreamer; that he was a man uncertain of himself and of his value and that as a result he needed to test himself, to pit himself against the most hideous environment and the most daunting task fortune could offer him. He was a solitary, facing his own mortality and the death of the whole world, setting against it nothing more than his own spirit and the efforts that this drove him to: in short, he was a romantic. It was the struggle he wanted, the hardship, the sense of loneliness and terror overcome. Nearly ten years before his death he had written, 'No journey ever made with dogs can approach the height of that fine conception which is realised when a party of men go forth to meet hardships, dangers and difficulties with their own unaided efforts, and by days and weeks of hard physical labour succeed in solving some problems of the great unknown.'

Afterwards came radios, aeroplanes, the paraphernalia of moonshots; from beyond their clutter his message still beckons, awakening some deep and atavistic, dormant layer of the soul. We nod, perhaps understanding for a moment the character of challenge and response; then too often turn away. But for Scott, in his era, it was a serious matter, it was the centre and purpose of his life. In the end it killed him.

Chronology

1868	6 June	Birth of Robert Falcon Scott
1883		Scott graduated from naval cadetship *Britannia*
1883-7		Scott served as midshipman
1887	14 August	Scott commissioned as sub-lieutenant
1891		Scott promoted to lieutenant
1897		Scott's father, John Scott, and his brother Archie both died
1900	9 June	Scott appointed commander of prospective Antarctic expedition
1900	June	Scott promoted to commander
1901	6 August	The *Discovery* sailed from Cowes
1902	3 January	The Antarctic circle was crossed
	9 January	The expedition landed at Cape Adare
	30 January	The expedition reached new land which Scott named King Edward VII Land
	4 February	Balloon ascent was made and the experiment abandoned
	8 February	The *Discovery* anchored in McMurdo Sound and the Hut Point site was chosen
	March/October	The expedition settled in winter quarters
	2 November	Scott's party set off south
	25 November	The party crossed the 80th parallel
	31 December	Scott, Wilson and Shackleton reached their furthest point south
1903	3 February	The party arrived back aboard the *Discovery*
	2 March	Relief ship *Morning* sailed from the Antarctic
	March/October	The party spent their second winter settled in quarters
	12 October	Scott's party set off westwards
	30 November	Scott, Petty Officers Evans and Lashly completed their outward journey
	December	The party arrived back aboard the *Discovery*
1904	5 January	Relief ships *Morning* and *Terra Nova* arrived
	16 February	The *Discovery* sailed for home after being ice-bound
	10 September	The *Discovery* arrived at Portsmouth
	10 September	Scott promoted to captain
1905	autumn	Scott's *The Voyage of the 'Discovery'* published
1906	August	Scott returned to the Navy
1908	2 September	Scott married Kathleen Bruce
1909	24 March	Scott appointed Naval Assistant to Second Sea Lord
	14 September	Birth of son Peter to the Scotts
	December	Scott resigned his Admiralty post to devote his time to prepare his second Antarctic expedition

	December	The *Terra Nova* purchased
1910	15 June	The *Terra Nova* sailed from Cardiff
	29 November	The *Terra Nova* sailed from Dunedin, New Zealand
1911	5 January	The expedition landed at Cape Evans and started to build winter quarters
	24 January	Scott's depot-laying party started out
	29 January	Safety Camp established
	29 January	The *Terra Nova* sailed for New Zealand
	17 February	One Ton Depot set up 670 miles from the Pole, the furthest point south before beginning the return journey ·
	22 February	The party reached Safety Camp. Scott learnt of the arrival of Amundsen and the Norwegian party in the Bay of Whales
	5 March	The split-up depot-laying party began converging on Hut Point, where they were then held up for four weeks
	8 April	Scott's party set off for the base at Cape Evans
	13 April	The party reached Cape Evans
	April/October	The expedition settled in winter quarters
	27 June/2 August	Wilson, Bowers and Cherry-Garrard made expedition to Cape Crozier to study the Emperor penguin
	1 November	Scott's party set out southwards
	21 November	Scott's party met up with the advance party at Mount Hooper
	9 December	The remaining ponies were killed
	14 December	Amundsen and the Norwegian party reached the South Pole
	22 December	The first returning party – Atkinson, Wright, Cherry-Garrard, Keohane – turned back
1912	4 January	The second returning party – Lieutenant Evans, Crean and Lashly – set off back
	17 January	The summit party – Scott, Wilson, Oates, Bowers and Petty Officer Evans – reached the Pole
	7 February	The party reached Upper Glacier Depot
	13 February	They arrived at Mid-Glacier Depot
	17 February	Petty Officer Evans collapsed and died
	2 March	The party reached Middle Barrier Depot
	15 March	Oates walked out into the snow to his death
	21 March	A 9-day blizzard began which snowed up Scott, Wilson and Bowers in their tent 11 miles from One Ton Depot
	29 March	Scott made the last entry in his diary
	12 November	The tent with the three men's bodies was found by the relief party

Select Bibliography

The Antarctic, H.G.R.King (Blandford Press. London, 1966)

Captain Scott, Stephen Gwynn (John Lane. London, 1929)

Diary of the 'Discovery' Expedition to the Antarctic 1901-1904, E.A.Wilson, edited by Ann Savours (Blandford Press. London, 1966)

The Lands of Silence, Sir Clements Markham (C.U.P. London, 1921)

Scott's Last Expedition, Captain R.F.Scott (Smith, Elder & Co. London, 1913)

Scott of the Antarctic, Reginald Pound (Cassell. London, 1966)

Shackleton, Margery and James Fisher (Barrie. London, 1957)

The South Pole, Roald Amundsen (John Murray. London, 1912)

South with Scott, E.R.G.R.Evans (Collins. London, 1921)

Under Scott's Command: Lashly's Antarctic Diaries, edited by Comdr. A.R.Ellis (Gollancz. London, 1969)

The Voyage of the 'Discovery', Captain R.F.Scott (Smith, Elder & Co. London, 1905)

The White Road, L.P. Kirwan (Hollis & Carter. London, 1959)

The Worst Journey in the World, A.Cherry-Garrard (Chatto & Windus. London, 1937)

Sir Thomas Moore

Acknowledgements

Photographs and illustrations were supplied by or are reproduced by kind permission of the following. The extracts from Captain Scott's diaries on pages 200–201 are reproduced by kind permission of Sir Peter Scott and the British Museum. British Antarctic Survey *180a* & *b*; British Museum 10–11, 13, 17, 19, 20; The Illustrated London News 38, 76, 77, 82, 92, 106–7, 112; The Mansell Collection 27, 106*l*, 197, 198; Mary Evans Picture Library 122: National Portrait Gallery 2, 16*l*, 103; New York Public Library *99a*; Norsk Polarinstitut 26; Popperfoto 31, 64, 65, 66, 86, 118–19, 126, 127, 132, 133, 134–5, 137, 138, 139, 141, 142, 143, 144–5, 148, 151, 153, *157a* & *b*, 158, 161, 162–3, 167, 168, 169, 171, 172–3, 182, 183, 191, 204–5, 210–11; The Press Association 49, 101, 114, 207; Radio Times Hulton Picture Library 16*r*, 22, 25, 28, 68, 71, 94–5, 97, 104, 109, 116, 120, 128, 152, 209; Royal Geographical Society 57, 82, 89, 90; Scott Polar Research Institute (no. 454) *3*, 14, (no. 538) *15a*, 15*b*, (no. 1335) 33, 34–5, (no. 56/27/12) 40–1, (no. 1333) 43, (no. 1462) *50*, (no. 1426) *51a*, (no. 480) *51b*, (no. 1290) 53, (no. 1374) 54, (nos. 1749, 67/4/2, 1459) 58, (no. 1394) 60, (no. 1903) *62*, (no. 1387) *62–3*, (no. 487) *63*, (no. 1761) 72–3, (no. 1336) 78, (no. 1460) 81, (no. 1342) 84, (no. 49/42) *98*, (no. 431) *99b*, (no. 1271) *110–11*, 125, 160, (no. 426) *177*, (no. 546) 179; Charles Swithinbank *189a* & *b*, *192a* & *b*; Victoria and Albert Museum 79.

Index